Pilgrimage

Patrick McCaskey

A Sports and Faith Series Book

Acts 12:1-2, Matthew 5:1-12, Acts 1:23-26, Acts 1:23-26, Luke 1:28-38, Matthew 1:20-21, Luke 1:39-45, Luke 1:46-55, 1 Samuel 2:30, 1 Timothy 4:6-8 *quotations are from The* Revised Standard Version Bible: Catholic Edition, copyright © 1989, 1993 the Division of Christian Education of the National Council of the Churches of Christ in the United States of America. Used by permission. All rights reserved.

Photographs appearing in *Pilgrimage* were sourced from Bear Woznick; Berthold Werner; Carmel High School; Carol Highsmith-Library of Congress; CBS; Donald Guthrie McNab; Fr. Lawrence Lew, O.P.; Frank Passi; Haley Scott DeMaria; Joshua Benoliel; Knock Shrine; LovesMacs; Patrick McCaskey; Paul Hermans; Sister Miriam James Heidland, S.O.L.T.; Sister Rita Clare Yoches; United States Army; U.S. State Department; and University of Notre Dame. Please see the Photographs and Illustrations Credit Table on pages 223-226 for more information.

The opinions and ideas expressed are those of the author who is entirely responsible for its content. The author has composed *Pilgrimage* at his own expense, using his own resources and technology. This publication is not associated in any way with the Chicago Bears Football Team.

Pilgrimage is Book 3 of the Sports and Faith Series.

CONTENTS

"The steel of manhood is tempered in the fire of adversity. Everybody has something wrong with them. Everyone's handicap is different because all of us are unique. When we are strong in an area in which others are weak, we are our brother's keeper."

—Edward McCaskey

Preface

Making a pilgrimage is a sacred, endearing, and social undertaking. The desire to take a pilgrimage is in our spiritual makeup. People are making pilgrimages, from long distance trips to short stops at local shrines. There are everyday pilgrimages to be taken as well. It might surprise you to think of it, but the Stations of the Cross at your local church is essentially a pilgrimage.

The Camino de Santiago or the Way of Saint James is the granddaddy of Christian Pilgrimages that requires a long trek. Featured in the movie, "The Way," it is something that we wanted to explore in this, our third book in the Sports and Faith Series. The "Camino" can be viewed like an athletic event; not a sports contest as such, but a religious experience that involves physical sacrifice, conditioning, and stamina. The Camino has many routes, but one of the most popular is a 500-mile trek that runs from the edge of southwestern France through the Pyrenees across the north of Spain. Today's adventurous Christians of all ages are putting the Camino on their bucket list.

Pilgrimages like the Camino often start out as a "find-myself" journey and end up surpassing all expectations. Travel on the Camino de Santiago has increased from a few hundred people in the 1980s to a quarter of a million today. Making the trek are people of all ages, but it's most comforting to see the young people blazing a trail for the future of the faith.

While researching for our third Sports and Faith Series book, we came across connections between the athletes we were examining and pilgrimages. We found connections to Lourdes, Fatima, Rome, Assisi, and other sacred places. Pilgrimages became the theme for the book. Every day we worked on this book, it become clearer that the notion of a "religious journey" is a perfect way to present our topic, sports and faith.

For Catholics, many pilgrimage sites are places of Marian Apparitions. The Catholic Church is careful about the endorsement of a Marian Apparition site. Even the language used to describe pilgrimage sites is fairly conservative. Places like Fatima and Lourdes are said to be "worthy of belief." The "worthy of belief" sites are certainly worthy of respect. The Church is not saying that you (if Catholic) have to believe in them, although obviously millions do, but the Church does not want any member to disparage them. Apparitions that happened a long time ago in out of the way places witnessed by children, may be difficult to believe for some. Yet, when faithful people gather in these places, worship God, and express themselves faithfully, they become truly holy places in every way.

On the Camino, the pilgrim often suffers hardships more than any other time in his or her life. Pilgrims make the trip in the company of thousands of other trekkers in various states of faith, and most believers go to Mass in the Cathedral of Saint James at the end of their trip. In places like Lourdes and Fatima, many pilgrims are deeply affected by the people there who are hurting and who are experiencing a healing in one way or another. Thousands of healthy people are witnesses and some aid the infirm. Crowds gather for various services and there are breathtaking candlelight processions. In Rome, pilgrims flock to the churches throughout the city, visit, and pray. In the Holy Land, pilgrims walk through narrow walkways where Jesus walked and they reflect on his sacrifice.

The belief in the sacred association of Jesus Christ, the Virgin Mary, and particular saints at pilgrimage sites varies greatly. It's not unusual for devout Christians to have their doubts about one site and at the same time believe deeply in the authenticity of another. In this book, the chapter openings that describe an individual pilgrimage or holy site tell of the events that have made it religious. We do not evaluate the site or shrine. At some sites, it may be unlikely that a review of "worthy of belief" or any other finding will ever be made—it will not be necessary. These sites are where the sacred are celebrated not necessarily where the celebrated were made sacred.

A shrine is a sacred place where the faithful make a pilgrimage for a particular reason, with the approval of the local ordinary.[1] A shrine does not necessarily have to be a place where miracles have occurred. At the North American Martyrs Shrine for example, there are no great designations at risk. It is the approximate site where martyrdom of North American missionaries took place. It is a place to honor those and others like them who were martyred as far away as Canada. That's not to say that healing and miracles are not associated with the martyrs, but the site honors the Martyrs' deeds and their attempts to spread the faith.

Once a pilgrimage experience is examined at the beginning of each chapter in this book, we have related stories of sports and faith. Like our two other Sports and

---

[1] Chester Gills, *Roman Catholicism in America* (New York: Columbia University Press, 1999) 158.

Faith Series books, *Pilgrimage* examines the lives of many athletes, coaches, and others who live exemplary lives. Often these people act courageously and unselfishly to help those who have the most difficult time in our society.

Many of the athletes described in this book are young. Here you will find future contributors and faithful servants. Their athletic preparation, discipline, conditioning, and spiritual and mental training will help them lead faithful lives, just as we need to live such lives as well. There are big shoes to fill as we go out to a world that was made better by so many great people.

People such as Father John Smyth, Father Ignatius McDermott, Wayne Gordon, Father Don Nevins, Stan Musial, George Halas, Art Rooney and others described in our Sports and Faith books followed a faith trail on their pilgrimage. Now younger trekkers will do the same. All of us labor each day on our continuing pilgrimage.

We hope our readers find the examples provided, both small and large, a source of inspiration. Perhaps that's the most attractive notion of this book; we are all on a pilgrimage, finding our way to God. And we are never alone.

Chapter 1: El Camino de Santiago

Pilgrimage is a term that calls to mind travel to holy places, prayer, witness, and worship. For many Christians, a pilgrimage may not involve the dusty travel and hardship it did for pilgrims long ago. A plane trip to Rome and a few days of visiting churches, the Vatican, and other holy places may be the trip of a lifetime but, it does not add up to the hardship other pilgrims experienced on sacred journeys that required hundreds of miles of travel on foot.

Most of us may never take a pilgrimage that involves a great journey. But the stories of such pilgrimages are inspiring. For those who may never be able to "make the trip," examples can move us as we travel on our own way.

You might remember the 2010 movie called "The Way." In it, Martin Sheen plays an ophthalmologist whose free-spirited son, played by Emilio Estévez (Sheen's own son), dies on his first day of pilgrimage. The Way or more formally "El Camino de Santiago de Compostela" (the way of Saint James in the field of stars) makes its path over the Pyrenees and across the northern part of Spain to the Cathedral of Saint James. Sheen takes the place of his son on the Camino and finishes a trek of discovery and faith. On the Camino, Sheen meets a number of other pilgrims who are everyday people, but who inspire us as they make their way.

There are many places where the Way may start, but the French Way, a very popular route, often begins in the French town of Saint-Jean-Pied-de-Port that is close to the Spanish border. The Sheens have roots in Spain in the vicinity of the Way. Martin's father was born in Parderrubias in Galicia—directly south of Santiago de Compostela. Martin's birth name was Ramón Antonio Gerardo Estévez. His father, Francisco Estévez, married an Irish woman, Mary Anne Phelan.

The Camino de Santiago pilgrimage has grown to a quarter of a million pilgrims in recent years. Books and films have been produced recently that promote the idea to people for many different reasons. Pilgrims may not often wear the large felt hat, dress in sandals or walk in bare feet, and carry a large crook with a hook to carry water, but you will often see them with modern backpacks that carry the traditional Camino symbol, the shell.

The Camino makes a big impression on pilgrims; they love to share their experiences. Many write that their lives have been divided into two parts, that part taking place before the Camino and that part after. It is that powerful. A pilgrimage that requires a physical component is something that appeals to people. Travel and exercise are certainly very popular these days. And young people today are brought up on more travel. Many take mission trips in their youth—so the Camino will grow for years to come.

In some ways, the popularity of the Way established a trekkers' brotherhood and sparked a recent mini-literary flowering. Yet, the journey received attention in the past as well. James Michener in his book *Iberia* (1968) discussed the Camino from a historical, cultural, and personal vantage point half a century ago.

Where great numbers venture out, much is written. During and after the Klondike Gold Rush, the subject of a recent PBS documentary, hundreds of books were written on the mining adventures of the participants.[2] And in some ways, religious pilgrims are seeking a treasure too, and wanting to experience the adventure that allures many.

The Camino is a sacred pilgrimage to many people; others make the trip as a type of meditation or a search for meaning. And yes, others are looking for the social or cultural experience. The Camino authorities encourage pilgrims to maintain a pilgrim's record book, have it stamped at various locations, and show it to officials at the end of the journey to obtain a certificate. Authorities give out one certificate to religious pilgrims and another to those who took the trip for non-religious reasons. Historically, Spain has been known for its strident faith, but little judgement is made on trekkers making the trip

---

[2] "The Klondike Gold Rush," for information see the PBS site at http://www.pbs.org/wned/klondike-gold-rush/home/.

today for any number of reasons. All are welcome on the Camino.

Origins

Apostles Saint James and his brother Saint John are called "Boanerges," in English, the "Sons of Thunder." This is due to their strong character and zeal, and their strong devotion to Jesus. Many believe their mother, Salome, was sister to the Virgin Mary. Herod Agrippa, grandson of Herod, had James beheaded on Passover 44 AD as part of Herod's attack against Christians.

"About that time Herod the king laid violent hands upon some who belonged to the church. He killed James the brother of John with the sword."

Acts 12:1-2

Saint Peter was seized shortly thereafter, but while in prison, he was freed by an angel. Peter survived decades longer and was martyred around 67 AD.

Many in Spain believe that James had worked there and he had converted many people. Some believe he was visited there by the Blessed Virgin Mary. Faith and tradition make the case for these events as hard evidence does not exist. James's remains were believed to be taken to Spain and buried in 44 AD around Iria Flavia, now called Padron.

Almost 800 years after James found rest in Spain, a hermit saw a star hovering over a field pointing to his burial site. The Saint's body was exhumed and moved to Compostela. Despite his martyrdom, James's body was non-corrupted (his head reattached and his remains intact). The Saint's presence would be needed. The Christians in Spain were battling the Muslims who had overtaken much of the "country" while displaying the arm of the Prophet Muhammad in battle.[3] After the discovery of James's body, he was seen at the head of the Christian army riding on a white horse. Under his influence, the Christians defeated the Muslims in Galicia. James was buried at Santiago de Compostela and he became the patron saint of Spain.

Other miracles have been attributed to Saint James. A bridegroom was swept into the sea and lost until his bride prayed to Saint James. The bridegroom was released from the sea covered in shells. The shell has become one of the symbols of the pilgrimage.

Pilgrimages began from different places in Europe and a Cathedral was built in Santiago. A French Priest named Aymeric Picaud wrote an early travel guide in mid-12th century called the *Codex Calixtinus* (the Manuscript of Pope Calixtus). The Pilgrim's Guide section was translated into English. According to James Michener in his book *Iberia*, Picaud set the standard for travel writers by praising people close to his home and criticizing those distant.

Interest in the Camino de Santiago has spawned a recent flowering of literature by a diverse group of pilgrims from movie stars to priests. One popular book is *Hiking the Camino* by a Franciscan priest, Father Dave Pivonka. Pivonka's book looks at the journey from the eyes of a priest at the 10th anniversary of his ordination. His story gives "pellegrino" wannabes a taste of the journey—sore feet and all—but it also examines the faith experience found along "the Way." It seems that each trekker's Camino experience is unique, but with some similarities. Some remind us of experiences that we

---

[3] Spain is used here to describe the area, but the actual country of Spain was not created until hundreds of years later. Likewise, the reconquest of Spain from Muslim to Christian hands took hundreds of years.

share with others on our own journey to Christ. There is something special about the Camino walk. Often, the mission achieves much more than most expect.

Saint Giles

Saint Giles lived in southern France. According to *Butler's Lives of the Saints*, Saint Giles was one of the more popular holy figures of the Middle Ages.[4] He lived from the mid-seventh to early eighth century.[5]

Saint Giles was a hermit saint. He lived on a Spartan diet and deer's milk. His reputation for piety made his recluse lifestyle impossible to maintain when followers joined him. He became an abbot.

Saint Giles was struck in the knee by an arrow that was shot by Wamba, a Visigoth King. Wamba was aiming at a deer who had befriended the Saint. Giles accepted his wound as an exercise in humility and suffering for the remainder of his life. King Wamba admired Giles. He gave Giles land that became the Abbey of Saint-Gilles-du-Gard. The abbey is on one of the official routes of the pilgrimage to Saint James. The city of Saint-Gilles-du-Gard is a World Heritage Site of the Routes of Santiago de Compostela. Known for his piety and fortitude, Saint Giles is the patron saint of the handicapped, lepers, and nursing mothers. Like many saints, much of what was written about Saint Giles was done hundreds of years

---

[4] The Middle Ages roughly lasted from the 5th to the 15th century. Some historians use the term Dark Ages to denote the earlier Middle Ages from the 5th to 10th century, but its use has declined recently.

[5] *Butler's Lives of the Saints* can be found in many different editions and readers have been educated and entertained on the book for generations. It was written in the mid-1700s. Irish writer Frank McCourt writes in *Angela's Ashes* that on a visit to the library on a rainy day, "I don't want to spend my life reading about saints but when I start (Butler) I wish the rain would last forever."

after his death and the facts are mixed with legend. Naturally, the deer is an animal with which the saint is often pictured. Saint Giles feast day is September 1st.

Saint Giles Parish

I spoke to the Men's Society at Saint Giles Parish in Oak Park, Illinois, at the invitation of Father Carl Morello and Pat Carew of the Society. Saint Giles is a parish that takes the work of their patron saint seriously and their effort reflects the blessing of Saint Giles:

Through the intercession of Saint Giles,

May our parish be a living witness of both prayer and compassion.

May we grow in respect for all of God's creation,

Especially the poor, the sick, the marginalized,

And those who have no voice.

And may we who bear the name of Saint Giles,

Also carry his gentle, healing and prayer-filled spirit to all of those in need.

We ask this through Christ, Our Lord. Amen.

Adventure on the Long Ride Home

EWTN TV and radio host, speaker, surfer, athlete and author, Bear Woznick is a "big surf dude with muscles" and much more. As Masters Tandem Surfing World Champion, he has developed tandem teams and events around the world. In tandem surfing, the male surfer lifts a woman while he is riding on the surfboard—the woman stands on his hands or shoulders, or she takes a different position that displays great control on both athlete's parts.

Woznick shares his love for surfing and for life in his book, *Deep in the Wave: A Surfing Guide to the Soul* (2012). For Bear, surfing is a metaphor for life, extreme sport is an expression of living life to the fullest, living life in faith. Woznick says living recklessly is living uninspired in mediocrity.

In Woznick's new book, *Deep Adventure: The Way of Heroic Virtue* (2016), Bear shares his real-life adventures as a way to challenge readers to go deeper with God and live a life of virtue. Pulse-pounding stories of ocean rescues, huge waves and deadly encounters with sharks show us that when people abandon themselves to God, they can live a life in pursuit of God's will in the boldest, most rewarding way possible.

Woznick is host of EWTN "Deep Adventure" radio show and producer, writer, and host of a new reality TV show: EWTN "Long Ride Home." In the first season of

"Long Ride Home," Woznick and a group of Christian men motorcycle across Texas sharing their spiritual thoughts and experiences with TV viewers. The show depicts Christian men who are unafraid and unapologetic about their faith while they display a heroic grit that is true masculine spirituality.

A serious adventure seeker, husband, father and devout Catholic, Bear's creed is "the most radical thing you can do in life is to abandon yourself to the wild adventure of God's will."

Woznick is an extreme athlete who has "Run with the Bulls" twice in Pamplona, the famous city that lies along the Way to Santiago. He has surfed world class waves and earned a ninja black belt. He encourages men to think of God's plan for their lives as one of action, he encourages men to be active for the faith and they will be more engaged in life, seeing and experiencing the beauty that God has created. In 2015, Woznick was inducted into the Sports Faith International Hall of Fame.

McCaskeys At Home

Many years ago, I wrote an essay about my family entitled "These Are My People." In the spring of 1974, Sue Rodelius (Dickson), Carol Reid (Nash), and I adapted it for the stage in an Oral Interpretation Class at Indiana University.

Bluebirds at Dinner

Dad finishes the prayer before dinner with a special plea for the Lord to "please convert the Russians."

Sue and Jim dive for the salad bowl. Sue gets it.

Dad says, "Treat your sister like a lady."

Jim replies, "When she acts like a lady, I'll treat her like one!"

Mom says, "Don't talk back to your father, Jim."

Jim replies, "I'm sorry. I guess the threat of nuclear war is getting to me."

Sue says, "I understand."

Barb says, "Dad, today we discussed Marshal McLuhan. He says that in the near future books will be obsolete because everybody will only watch television. What do you think?"

Sue and Jim make disgusted faces at each other while Barb is talking.

Dad replies, "Well, I've always enjoyed reading and I think I always will."

Barb says, "But Dad, how can you enjoy reading in this house? If it's not the dogs, it's the stereo or the 'boob tube.'"

Dad replies, "Television has not made reading obsolete any more than the printing press made conversation obsolete."

Barb says, "But it sure makes reading difficult."

Sue and Jim lean over their plates and sneer and pick at their food. Sue catches Mom's eye and quickly takes her elbows off the table. Jim immediately follows. Jim sees Dad's glare and snaps to attention. Sue does too.

Dad and Mom wink at each other. Sue is again lost in thought.

Dad says, "Speaking of books, Jim, how's school coming?"

Jim looks sheepish.

PILGRIMAGE

Mom says, "We got your quarter grades today." There was a long pause and Sue snickers.

Dad says, "There was an interesting note at the bottom; it seems that you have set a school record. This teacher feels, if you graduate, you will hold the record for the greatest number of detentions that will probably never be broken."

Sue bursts out laughing.

Dad continues, "However, Sonny Boy, I've signed the report anyway."

Jim takes the report card and reads, "Jim only got a D last quarter in your course. I think you're a better teacher than that and so I'm going to give you another chance to prove yourself."

Jim says, "I don't like teachers who dissect stories to find the symbolic messages."

Barb says, "Isaac Bashevis Singer says that the only message writers should have is The Ten Commandments."

Mom replies, "That's a wonderful idea, but I'm sure Mister Singer expressed it with proper grammar."

Barb says, "Excuse me. Isaac Bashevis Singer says the only messages that writers should have are The Ten Commandments. Thank you Mom."

Sue looks very put out. She sees a spoon in her hand that she throws at Jim. This starts a wrestling match between them.

Barb asks, "Why don't we separate the babies?"

She does this by sitting between them. Sue and Jim look disgusted.

Mom says, "Ed, I had to call the plumber again about the upstairs toilet."

Dad asks, "Just the upstairs?"

Mom replies, "Yes Edward."

Dad says, "What do you want? Two out of three working is pretty good."

Sue asks, "What was the plumber's symbolic message, Jim?"

Jim begins to snap back, but he can't think of anything.

Mom replies "That plumbers make more money than English teachers."

All do a take to Mom who is obliviously eating.

Dad asks, "Jim, was that you I heard coming in at 12:00 last night? I thought I told you to be in by 11:00."

Jim replies, "Uh...well...uh...I was home by 11:00. I just went out to close the garage door at 12:00. I didn't do it before because I was saying my rosary."

Dad says, "I want you to watch out for young women who are interested in you, just to become my daughter-in-law."

Jim replies, "Yes sir."

Mom says, "Your father is a very compassionate person. When we were getting married, he was very concerned about all the possible suicides."

Jim replies, "That was very humane, Dad."

Dad says, "When I was 17, my hair turned curly just like yours son. God I was good looking. The girls didn't have a chance."

Jim asks, "How did you handle it, Dad?"

Dad replies, "I watched out for the web-weavers, those young women who are merely interested in getting married. When I told one of them that it was over, she fainted. A month later she was engaged to someone else."

Sue bursts out laughing and spews milk all over the table and everyone.

Dad asks, "All right what's going on?"

Jim replies, "Nothing." Jim glares at Sue. Obviously something is wrong.

Dad says, "Sue, you tell me."

Sue replies, "Uh...well...um..."

Barb asks, "Dad, may I say something?"

Dad replies, "Sure Barb."

Barb says, "Well I'd like to say that I feel – I feel I'd like to wipe off all the milk that Sue spit all over me."

All laugh. Barb realizes that she is funny and she smiles for the first time in ten years.

Dad looks at his watch and says, "Better hurry if we're going to catch the sports: ready break." After the children leave the table, Dad says to Mom, "Laughing Girl, to be a father you have to be a Solomon."

Dad and Mom say together, "No two kids are alike."

The Annunciation

Chapter 2: The Holy Land

The United States Conference of Catholic Bishops reminds us that the Church of Jerusalem was the Mother Church for us all. It guided the faithful. It was from Jerusalem that the apostles went forth to spread the gospel. A few million Christians make a pilgrimage to the Holy Land each year and many start with Jerusalem. The Holy Land includes Israel, the Palestinian Territories, Jerusalem, and Jordan. It's a politically complicated area and the pilgrimage sights reflect the repeated building and rebuilding of area churches.

Like many Christian practices, a pilgrimage to the Holy Land, more specifically, Jerusalem, was a practice the Jews encouraged their people to make. In fact, the Jews often made three pilgrimages a year to Jerusalem: One for Passover; a second one for Shavuot, to commemorate the gift of the 10 Commandments; and a third for Sukkot, to commemorate the wanderings in the desert.[6]

Jerusalem is located between the Mediterranean and the Dead Sea. It is one of the oldest cities in the world and is sacred to three major religions: Judaism, Christianity, and Islam. Israelis and Palestinians both claim Jerusalem as their capital.

Christian pilgrimages and tours of the Holy Land often include some or all of 10 sites: Church of All Nations, Church of the Holy Sepulchre, Basilica of the Annunciation, Christian sites in Jerusalem, Garden of Gethsemane, Garden Tomb, Mount of Beatitudes, Mary's Tomb, Tabgha, and the Via Dolorosa.[7]

Tabgha is a name most Christians have not heard. Tabgha is the location of a famous miracle depicted in the New Testament, the multiplication of loaves and fishes. The Church of the Multiplication of the Loaves and Fishes was destroyed in the seventh century and restored recently to its Byzantine form, incorporating portions of the original mosaics found on the site.

A fourth-century woman named Egeria wrote one of the oldest existing accounts of a pilgrimage to the Holy Land. What has survived of Egeria's account indicates that she took a long and expensive journey by herself and visited many places. She is thought to have been a well-educated woman, perhaps a nun from Europe. Her descriptions of the liturgy used in the Holy Land at the time have been most helpful to the Church. Her writings were followed by other pilgrims' writings in the coming years.

---

[6] George Weigle, *Roman Pilgrimages: The Station Churches* (New York: Basic Books, 2003).

[7]. Holy Land Voyager web site at: http://www.tourstotheholyland.com

The Crusades to the Holy Land began in the 11ᵗʰ century and continued into the 13ᵗʰ. Crusades throughout the years were sometimes noble and sometimes ignoble. Originally supported by the Western and the Eastern Church, the later Crusades were led by Europeans with mixed motives.

Church of the Holy Sepulchre

The Church of the Holy Sepulchre in the Old City of Jerusalem encompasses the site of Calvary, where Jesus was crucified, and the Holy Sepulchre, where Jesus was buried before he rose from the dead. Early Christian liturgies were held there until the Romans took the city in 66 AD. In 135 AD, Emperor Hadrian buried the site to build a temple to Aphrodite, the Greek Goddess of Love and Beauty.[8]

Emperor Constantine started to uncover the site to build the Church of the Holy Sepulchre in 326 AD. Builders exposed the tomb and built the Church around it, which was formally dedicated in 335. Constantine's mother, Saint Helena, discovered what was said to be the True Cross near the tomb.

The Church of the Holy Sepulchre was damaged by fire in 614 AD and was reconstructed. In 638, the Christians surrendered Jerusalem to Muslim caliph Omar. The Church continued to function as a Christian church until 1009, when Fatimid caliph Hakim destroyed it, knocking over the walls and attacking the tomb of Christ. Much was lost, but some was protected by rubble. The church was partially rebuilt, but was still in disarray when the First Crusade took place in 1096-

---

[8] Hadrian also built a temple in Rome to Venus (Rome's version of Aphrodite) and Roma.

1099. The church was slowly renovated throughout the 1100s.

Greek Orthodox, Armenian Apostolic, and Roman Catholic churches have responsibilities for the church. Also involved are the Coptic Orthodox, the Ethiopian Orthodox and the Syrian Orthodox. Poor repairs, another fire, and an earthquake caused further damage over the centuries. In 1959, the three major responsible communities (Latins, Greeks, and Armenians) agreed on a renovation plan, but the results are not impressive. Visitors see a dissimilarly decorated church. Never-the-less, many pilgrims give their attention to the religious meaning of the site.

Basilica of the Annunciation

Basilica of the Annunciation

A Basilica is located at the site of the Annunciation in Nazareth. The current 1969 church was built over the sites of earlier churches. The lower level contains the

Grotto of the Annunciation, the remains of the home of Mary.

The first shrine was built in the cave in which Mary had lived. A larger church was commissioned by Emperor Constantine. Constantine's church was destroyed in the seventh century after a Muslim conquest. A crusaders' church replaced Constantine's building. Another Muslim conquest took place in 1102, but the Franciscans were allowed to keep the church in operation. In 1260, a tall fair-skinned blue-eyed Turk named Baybars and his Mamluk army destroyed the church during their attack on Nazareth.[9] A small number of Franciscans managed to stay in Nazareth until the fall of crusader-controlled Acre in 1291. Acre was the last Christian outpost of significant strength and its fall signaled the end of the great European vision of a Christian-controlled Middle East.

In the three centuries that followed, the Franciscans were in and out of Nazareth. The Franciscans were expelled in 1363 and they returned in 1468, but some members were massacred in 1542. In 1730, the church was rebuilt and the Franciscans still managed to look after it. The church was demolished again in 1954, this time not by soldiers, but by builders who replaced it with the present building completed in 1969. The new basilica was designed by Italian architect Giovanni Muzio and built by construction firm Solel Boneh. It remains under the control of the Franciscans. It is the largest Christian sanctuary in the Middle East, and it was dedicated in 1964 by Pope Paul VI (1963-1978).

The Basilica houses mosaics of Marian devotions from different countries. The modern Church of the

---

[9] Mamluk armies were Moslem armies that were populated by slaves and were used during the Middle Ages.

Annunciation features a concrete dome and an upper church and a lower church.

Tabgha

Tabgha, formerly known as Heptapegon, is a small area on the northwest shore of the Sea of Galilee where the fishing is exceptionally good. Tabgha is where the miracle of loaves and fishes occurred. The Church of the Multiplication of Loaves and Fishes in Tabgha commemorates the miraculous feeding of the five thousand hungry pilgrims who came to hear Jesus.

A church of the Feeding of the Five Thousand was first built here in 350 and enlarged in 480. It had beautiful mosaics. It was destroyed in 685 AD. The site was excavated in 1932 and the mosaics were preserved. In 1982, a modern Church of the Multiplication of the Loaves and Fishes was built.

Mount of Beatitudes

Near the Church of Loaves and Fishes, the Mount of Beatitudes is commemorated with another church. According to author Lynn Austin, "The Church of the Beatitudes preaches like a queen on top of a hill overlooking the Sea of Galilee."[10] The church was constructed on the ruins of a fourth-century Byzantine church. The new octagon-shaped church was designed by Italian architect Antonio Barluzzi. Barluzzi built or restored churches, hospitals, and schools in the Holy Land in the first half of the 20th century.[11] Each side of

---

[10] Lynn Austin, *Pilgrimage: My Journey to a Deeper Faith in the Land Where Jesus Walked* (Minneapolis: Bethany House, 2013) 191.

[11] "Antonio Barluzzi, an architect in the Holy Land," on Custodia Terrae Sanctae, web site of the Franciscan Missionaries Serving the Holy Land,

the church contains a window on which one of the Beatitudes is printed in Latin.

The Beatitudes

Seeing the crowds, he went up on the mountain, and when he sat down his disciples came to him. And he opened his mouth and taught them, saying:

"Blessed are the poor in spirit, for theirs is the kingdom of heaven.

Blessed are those who mourn, for they shall be comforted.

Blessed are the meek, for they shall inherit the earth.

Blessed are those who hunger and thirst for righteousness, for they shall be satisfied.

Blessed are the merciful, for they shall obtain mercy.

Blessed are the pure in heart, for they shall see God.

Blessed are the peacemakers, for they shall be called sons of God.

Blessed are those who are persecuted for righteousness' sake, for theirs is the kingdom of heaven.

Blessed are you when men revile you and persecute you and utter all kinds of evil against you falsely on my account. Rejoice and be glad, for your reward is great in heaven, for so men persecuted the prophets who were before you."

—Matthew 5:1-12

---

viewed at http://www.custodia.org/default.asp?id=779&id_n=1071 on May 31, 2016.

Via Dolorosa

Via Dolorosa is the "Way of Grief," a path in the Old City of Jerusalem where Jesus was led to his crucifixion. It starts from the place where Jesus was tried and convicted, which is near the Lions' Gate, and it ends in the crucifixion place, Golgotha, inside the Church of the Holy Sepulcher.[12] The 14 Stations of the Cross are marked along the way.

---

12 The Old City of Jerusalem was surrounded by walls that date back to the rule of the Ottoman Sultan Suleiman the Magnificent. The Lions Gate is one of 11 gates to the city and has images of lions on its crest.

Joseph-Barsabbas-Justus

"And they put forward two, Joseph called Barsabbas, who was surnamed Justus, and Matthias. And they prayed and said, 'Lord, who knowest the hearts of all men, show which one of these two thou hast chosen to take the place in this ministry and apostleship from which Judas turned aside, to go to his own place.' And they cast lots for them, and the lot fell on Matthias; and he was enrolled with the eleven apostles."

Acts 1:23-26

After Jesus had ascended
To heaven,
Peter quarterbacked the replacement
Of Judas.
Joseph-Barsabbas-Justus and Matthias
Were the two finalists.
The Apostles prayed
For guidance
And then had the coin-toss.
Saul had won a similar toss
To become the first king
Of Israel
About 1000 B.C.
Matthias won this toss
To become the twelfth Apostle.
"There had
To be twelve
To correspond
To the twelve tribes
Of Israel." ("Who's Who in the Bible")
Roger Staubach wore number 12.
Perhaps it was Joseph-Barsabbas-Justus
Who invented the concept
Of a baker's dozen.

22

Joseph-Barsabbas-Justus persevered;
He became a saint.
— Patrick McCaskey

The Church of All Nations

The Church of All Nations is located on the Mount of Olives in Jerusalem, next to the Garden of Gethsemane. Today's church was built with funds from many different countries; certainly a remarkable accomplishment that gave the shrine its current name. Previously, it had been called the Basilica of the Agony. The church rests on the foundations of two earlier ones: one 12th century crusader chapel and a fourth-century Byzantine basilica, destroyed by an earthquake in 746. Work on the current basilica took place from 1922-1924. Violet covered glass conjures the somber mood of the Mount of Olives in the church and the ceiling is painted deep blue.

The front facade of the church includes a modern mosaic panel depicting Jesus Christ as mediator between God and man. The mosaic is supported by a row of Corinthian columns. The designer of the mosaic was Giulio Bargellini. The church itself was designed by Italian architect Antonio Barluzzi.

New Crusader Wants to Help Others

Crusader structures were built in the Holy Land often to replace or restore older structures. Visitors are reminded of the crusaders history. Recently, much has been written on the Crusades.

Today's "crusaders" are just as devoted to doing God's will as those early adventurers. They are health care workers, social service workers, educators, military personnel, and more. Today's crusaders often begin their early lives as athletes, where conditioning, training, and contests prepare them for future pursuits.

April Ortenzo is an outstanding athlete and a modern-day crusader. At Cardinal Gibbons High School, Fort Lauderdale, Florida, she was the starting shortstop who led the varsity team in hitting and received the Outstanding Player Award each year since her freshman year. For 3 years she placed in the top ten hitters in Broward County and she graduated with a 4.05 GPA.

She served as coach for the Cardinal Gibbons sports camps (baseball, softball, soccer) and participated in the Fellowship of Christian Athletes. She was a member of Mary Help of Christians Church in Parkland, Florida. Looking forward to the future, she said: "My main goal in life is to help other people. I feel it is what I am meant to do." April Ortenzo was named America's Catholic High School Female Athlete of the Year by *USA Today* and she was awarded the Sports Faith International Award for Female Athlete of the year.

Ortenzo fielded a boat-load of scholarship offers and chose West Point, the United States Military Academy. Playing for the Black Knights, she started in 223 games during her 4-year career and served as team captain in her junior and senior years. She is among the academy's all-time top five in at-bats, hits, doubles, RBIs, runs, and stolen bases. She holds a .966 fielding percentage at shortstop. After graduation, she stayed on at West Point as a graduate assistant for a semester.

Ortenzo is currently stationed at Joint Base Lewis-McChord, Washington, and she still plays ball. The Second Lieutenant serves on the All-Army Women's

April Ortenzo

Softball Team. The All-Army Team went a perfect 9-0 in a tournament with wins over Air Force, Navy, and the Marines at Marine Corps Base at Camp Lejeune, North Carolina—winning the 2015 Armed Forces Softball Championship. Ortenzo was named to the All-Tournament Team and she was chosen to play on the All-Armed Forces Team in Oklahoma City. Ortenzo not only won her second gold medal of the season in Oklahoma City, she was named the tournament's Most Valuable Player, and her team won the American Softball Association national crown.

"I grew up in a disciplined household," Ortenzo said. "My parents were both police officers. My brother is a police officer. I knew that whatever school or path I chose that I wanted to serve in some way, shape or form, whether police force, firefighter, or the military."[13]

Soldiers with Gifts from God

Coaches must be crusaders for their programs and their athletes. In top high school sports programs, coaches face many expectations. Many parents and athletes focus on how a player is featured on a team. Do they get enough time in the limelight? Are their skills front and center for college scouts? As a program gets more successful, a head coach must also manage a greater number of assistant coaches, and operate in a more complex environment. It is not easy!

Head Football Coach Steve Specht and Cincinnati Saint Xavier High School administrators focus on the player's character—seeing an individual develop into a better man. Help "build great kids" first and worry about winning second. Specht believes high school coaches better be "all about the kids."

Specht has three principles for success that he shares with his team: 1). Love one another. 2). Be the best you can be. 3). Lean on one another when times get tough. These principles at Specht's Jesuit school have produced much fruit. Specht's Xavier Bombers play in one of the toughest state high school football divisions in the country. Although they have two State Championships, every season is a new challenge. Once the season starts, there are weekly visits of the team to the chapel; daily readings connect in a meaningful way to the lives of the players. Everything is a gift from God and one that each player should appreciate.

---

[13] Official web page of United States Army viewed at http://www.army.mil/article/157913/Dad_proud_of_daughter_s_choi ce_to_play_softball_for_Army/ on December 29, 2015.

PILGRIMAGE

Specht loves to share the story from Matthew 25:14 regarding talents. He uses this to express his belief that each player is given talents from the Lord. Those with greater talents are asked to use them often for the success of the team. For those with undeveloped talents, or talents that lie in other areas, he offers his commitment and that of the other coaches to lead a player to his full potential.

Specht uses football to teach what is important in life and how to live it, so that it honors the Lord. He urges his players to look in the mirror each night and ask, "Am I better today?" If they can answer yes, wonderful, keep forging ahead. If the answer is no, they need to figure out why and commit to turning it around the next day.

Specht has been doing what his coaches did for him many years ago. He's been blessed, but many obstacles taught him lessons about faith and what he needs to do for others. Specht believes everything has its place in this world including winning and losing. He believes it is easier to learn after wins, but it's a true test of character to be able to pick up and learn from your mistakes when you lose. It's important to learn from both. In winning, players need to learn how to maintain a strong sense of humility; how to be grateful for all of the gifts they have been given; and understand how to work hard each day to be their best. They need to respond to new challenges and each game presented is an opportunity to compete to the best of their abilities and, God willing, end up on the winning side of the scoreboard. Mostly they need to learn that being a champion is not about winning football games, but about being the best possible individual every day of their lives.

Specht has been named the Don Shula NFL High School Coach of the Year, the Cincinnati Bengals Paul Brown Excellence in Coaching Award recipient, and the

Sports Faith International Catholic High School Coach of the Year.

Perfect Pilgrimage

Michigan forests were harvested and sent down the Muskegon River to Muskegon Lake, which is connected to Lake Michigan by a channel. Fur trapping and trading were important. The lumber industry made Muskegon the "Lumber Queen of the World." Today it is a progressive city with excellent schools, many industries, great outdoor activities, and natural beauty.

High School Head Football Coach Mike Holmes finished 25 seasons at Muskegon Catholic Central and retired at the end of the 2013 school year. Holmes finished with six State Championships. Holmes's teams were disciplined. Holmes was described as ethical and principled—totally committed to getting the most and the best from his football team.

Called by the Muskegon Chronicle as "nothing short of a coaching genius," Holmes's overall record of 278 victories, 80 losses, and one tie has earned him Muskegon Area Sports Hall of Fame Award, the State of Michigan Football Coach of the Year Award from the Michigan High School Coaches Association, and the Sports Faith International Hall of Fame Award. Holmes worked for 33 years in Catholic Education; in addition to football coach, he served as a teacher, athletic director, and principal. During his years at MCC, Holmes saw to it that a team Rosary and Mass were offered before every game. He brought with him a deep heritage of Catholic faith and he served as a Eucharistic Minister. He and his coaches were sticklers for fundamentals and preparation—each play was drilled until perfect. Holmes is a man whose faith is the engine to his long success.

Lafayette Pilgrims that Give Back

The importance of giving back is manifested when the Lafayette Central Catholic Baseball Team hosts a two-day Christmas Baseball Camp for all the youth in the community. The players serve as coaches, instructors, and mentors. They emphasize the importance of commitment, integrity, teamwork, and competing in a Christ-like manner.

Sports Faith International named the Lafayette Central Catholic Baseball Team to its Hall of Fame after the team won the 2009 Indiana State Championship. Since 2000, Lafayette has been state champion seven times. Coach and Athletic Director Tim Bordenet was the youngest coach named into the Indiana Baseball Hall of Fame in 2012. Many of Bordenet's players are involved with school leadership groups and important co-curricular activities. Despite the exceptional record for sports and scholarship at Lafayette Central Catholic, back in 1990 a decision was made to close the school.

Parents and community responded and a successful financial plan was implemented to save it. Since then, the Lafayette Central Catholic community continues extraordinary efforts to support the school and keep it successful in every way possible.

Saint Peter's Dome

Chapter 3: Rome

While many Christian pilgrims had their sights set on the Holy Land, it was not always a safe destination. Pilgrimages to Rome grew more popular. In Rome, pilgrims can see art, architecture, relics, tombs, literature, and sacred sights. At the same time, visitors can participate in Papal audiences, Papal weekly addresses, and the day-to-day business of the Vatican and churches throughout the city. Pilgrims can also pray and attend Mass at any number of beautiful historic churches.

Traditional Roman pilgrimage sights are the seven pilgrim basilicas that are deemed major. Four are papal basilicas: Saint Peter, Saint John Lateran, Saint Mary Major, and Saint Paul Outside the Walls. The other major basilicas are Saint Lawrence Outside the Walls,

Holy Cross in Jerusalem (yes, this church is in Rome), and Saint Sebastian.

During Jubilee Years or Holy Years, visits to the papal basilicas can lead to indulgences. The Popes have established standard periods of time between such years, but "extraordinary" years have also been made Holy Years. The pope issues a Bull (official document) on the celebration with a starting and ending date. Symbols help pilgrims to celebrate the Holy Year and direct pilgrims to a deeper experience. At the basilicas, a sealed Holy Door is opened to begin a Holy Year. Roman pilgrims come to the basilicas to venerate the sacred, to do penance, and to give thanks.

Saint Peter's Basilica: The Finest Thing in the Universe

Emperor Constantine built many Christian churches. He built the original Saint Peter's Basilica from 326-333 AD, a church which we associate with the Pope today. However, Constantine's Saint John Lateran Basilica was the Pope's church and the Lateran Palace his home. The churches built by Constantine continue to operate over the years. Their histories reflect the rocky story of the Church, which survives with the aid and mercy of God.

People point out that in our imperfect world, God's hand helps lead the Church through troubled times and good times as well. When you read the history of the Church, some of the most difficult times occurred when political and sometimes national encroachment took place. Certainly, the tempestuous times in the 1300s in Europe reflect this. History reveals the imperfect effort of man and the perfect steering of God directing the Church back on course.

31

King Philip IV of France was an ambitious king who ruled from 1285-1314. He took steps to control the feudal lords of France; to put the church leaders in France under his control; to eliminate the Knights Templar and therefore the debt owed to them; and to spread his influence throughout Europe.

Phillip was at odds with Pope Boniface VIII (1294-1303) who many historians suggest had his own struggles with power.[14] Pope Boniface is remembered in part for the first Jubilee Year of 1300 at which he proclaimed a plenary indulgence for pilgrims who visited the Apostles' Basilicas, Saint Peter's Basilica, and the Basilica of Saint Paul Outside the Walls in the state of true penitence.[15] The practice would be sustained in other Holy Years and evolved to include visits to Saint John Lateran Basilica and Saint Mary Major Basilica in 1400.

King Philip's clash with Pope Boniface came to a head and the King sent men who seized the Pope in France and imprisoned him. This rough treatment likely resulted in his death. Pope Benedict XI (1303-1304) succeeded Boniface, but he died after 8 months of taking office. At the time, there was a power struggle in the hierarchy of the Church. Under Phillip's influence, Pope Clement V (1305-1314), a Frenchman was elected in 1305. Pope Clement immediately added many French cardinals and the Church was in for a long period of French influence throughout the century. Pope Clement decided he was not going to Rome and moved the papal

[14] Morris Bishop, *The Middle Ages* (Boston: Houghton Mifflin, 1968) 301.
[15] Catholic Encyclopedia indicates a plenary indulgence as the remission of the entire temporal punishment due to sin so that no further expiation is required in Purgatory. (See their coverage at http://www.newadvent.org/cathen/07783a.htm)

residence to Avignon in 1309. A line of French Popes were subsequently elected. The Papacy remained in France for 67 years and the French royalty exerted influence. While Clement eventually approved of the seizure and trial of the Templars, it was the King who was behind it.[16] In other ways however, Clement tried to work around outside influence when it might have resulted in permanent injury to the Church.

It was Pope Gregory XI (1370-1378) who left Avignon and returned to Rome on January 17, 1377. After Gregory's death, a little over a year after his return to Rome, Pope Urban VI (1378-1389) was elected and immediately began criticizing the French Cardinals, the gifts they received, and their lifestyle. The French Cardinals called the Pope's election illegitimate and the Western Schism was born leading to a line of antipopes that lasted until 1417 when the Council of Constance took place.

The old Saint Peter's Basilica fell into disrepair along with other churches in Rome when the papacy was in France. The Western Schism affected a rebirth in the Church and its buildings in Rome on an unimaginable scale. A new Saint Peter's Basilica was begun in 1506, finished over a hundred years later in 1614 and consecrated on November 18, 1626. Under Pope Julius II (1503-1513), Donato Bramante was made chief architect, but that role was most notably taken over by Michelangelo in 1547 and finished by others. During the construction, 21 popes and 8 architects were involved plus several of the greatest artists of the time. The building of Saint Peter's Basilica was a project of such

---

[16] Duc De Castries, *The Lives of the Kings & Queens of France* (New York: Alfred A. Knopf, 1979) 92.

size and scope that it became a metaphor for "never-ending projects."

Saint Peter's Basilica was cruciform, formed like a cross. It was at times designed in the model of a Greek cross, where the nave (main body of the church), chancel (the space around the altar) and transept arms (an area set crosswise to the naive in a cruciform church) are of equal length. But the church was finished in the Latin cross plan. It was the largest Christian church for many centuries. The art treasuries, sacred burial place of popes, the many chapels, and other wonders made it a popular place of pilgrimage.

Various Popes oversaw the building of the new Saint Peter's Basilica. Their mission incurred the criticism of historians, theologians, and writers. Martin Luther began the Protestant Reformation in 1517 while the Basilica was being built. Yet, despite the errors of many and the continuing changes in leadership, Saint Peter's Basilica has been called the "finest thing in the universe."[17]

Saint John Lateran

Emperor Constantine had a vision the night before he was to defeat his main rival, Emperor Maxentius, north of Rome in 312 AD. He saw a cross of light and heard a voice say: "In this sign you shall conquer."[18] Constantine would convert to Christianity and would approve the Christian faith via the Edict of Milan in 313. Afterwards, Constantine gave the Lateran Palace

---

[17] Words of 18th century traveler Charles de Brosses, see June Hager, *Pilgrimage: A Chronicle of Christianity Through the Churches of Rome* (London: Weidenfeld & Nicolson, 1999) 189-190.

[18] Joan Lewis, *A Holy year in Rome* (Manchester, NH: Sophia Institute Press, 2015) 81.

and grounds to the Catholic Church and ordered that a basilica be built on the property dedicated to the Redeemer or Most Holy Savior. The Palace's horse guards barracks were raised to build the first basilica in Rome, which Constantine wanted to be the greatest of all churches. Consecrated in 324, Saint John Lateran underwent many disasters and revivals.[19] Known today as the Archbasilica of Saint John Lateran, it is the Pope's official church, the Cathedral of the Bishop of Rome. The Lateran Palace was the pope's official residence for 1000 years until the late 14th century. The church is the only cathedral in Rome; a church which contains a Bishop's throne. The church was newly dedicated to Saint John the Baptist and to Saint John the Evangelist in the 12th century. These dedications gave the church its new name: Saint John Lateran.[20]

Saint John Lateran

---

[19] June Hager, *Pilgrimage: A Chronicle of Christianity Through the Churches of Rome* (London: Weidenfeld & Nicolson, 1999) 203.

[20] The churches that have existed for many centuries were rebuilt over time and in some cases even the names have changed or evolved. Many also have a short-hand name that may be different than the actual name.

When the Popes returned to Rome from Avignon, Saint John Lateran Basilica was in disrepair and the Pope moved shortly thereafter to the Vatican and Saint Peter's. Pope Sixtus V (1585-1590) tore down Saint John Lateran Basilica and its buildings and replaced them with late Renaissance structures designed by Domenico Fontana. The interior design was subsequently transformed for the Jubilee in 1650. The exterior facade was replaced in 1735.

Saint Mary Major

Saint Mary Major is the greatest Roman church honoring the Lord's mother. Saint Mary Major has two stories of origin. The current Saint Mary Major was completed after the Council of Ephesus of 431 by Pope Sixtus III (432-440) to honor the Virgin Mary who the Council had proclaimed Mary Mother of God. But many years before the council, a remarkable shared vision had established the site of the original church.

A Roman from the ruling class and his wife had been praying faithfully for guidance on what to do with their fortune since they had no children. On August 4, 358, in a dream, the Virgin Mary appeared to the couple and asked them to build a church in her honor where snow would fall that night. The following morning on August 5, they rushed off to confer with Pope Liberius (352–366), who revealed that he had the same dream! That day, snow was found on one of Rome's seven hills, Esquiline. The Pope, the patrician couple, and others went out to mark the location. A basilica was built on this site called Our Lady of the Snows—otherwise known as the Liberian Basilica (for the Pope's involvement) and later, Saint Mary Major. Each year on August 5, during

Mass in Saint Mary Major Basilica, a shower of white rose petals falls from an opening in the ceiling above the altar to commemorate the snowfall in 358.

For the Roman people, Saint Mary Major Basilica is especially significant and home to one of the most important icons. A painting of Mary on wood called the Protectorate (or Salvation) of the Roman people, Madonna Salus Populi Romani, is housed in the Borghese Chapel in the Basilica. Pope Francis, who was elected in 2013, has been to the Basilica to offer prayers immediately after his election, to pray there before his trip to Brazil, and to open the Holy Door there to signal the Jubilee of Mercy.[21]

Saint Mary Major Basilica also houses relics from the crib of Jesus—boards of sycamore wood brought to the church in 642 at the time of Pope Theodore I (642-649). Magnificent mosaics on the Ephesus Triumphal Arch above and behind the main altar are especially admired. The remains of Saint Jerome, the great Biblical scholar, are here. Like all of the Roman churches, pilgrims and tourists can spend many hours praying, seeing, and admiring the site. The basilica was restored, redecorated, and extended by Pope Eugene III (1145-1153), Pope Nicholas IV (1288–92), Pope Clement X (1670–76), and Pope Benedict XIV (1740–58). Outside the Basilica is a six story bell tower.

Saint Paul Outside the Walls

The site of Saint Paul's burial was a popular place to visit since the day he died. The Papal Basilica, Saint Paul Outside the Walls, was built over the burial place

---

[21] These are not Pope Francis's only visits to the church.

of Saint Paul, completed in 324 AD.[22] It was another church ordered built by Emperor Constantine. But the church itself proved inadequate for the large number of visitors. In 386 AD, Emperor Valentinian II razed Constantine's Basilica and built a larger version.[23]

The church underwent many improvements over the years, but in 1823, it was destroyed by fire. Pope Leo XII (1823-1829) encouraged donations for reconstruction and the new church was opened in 1840 after assistance came from many places from many faiths. The new basilica maintains the original plan and it is one of the largest churches in Rome. A fifth century Apse (semicircular section that comes at the end of the aisles) covered in Mosaic images was saved from the Valentinian structure and is one of the most admired parts of the church.

The outside area of the church is beautiful. A large portico with 150 columns and a statue of Saint Paul greets visitors. Visitors express particular affection for

[22] The Basilica is "Outside the Walls" in that it is two kilometers outside the Aurelian Walls surrounding Rome.

[23] Frank J. Korn, *A Catholic's Guide to Rome* (New York: Paulist Press, 2000) 67.

the peaceful cloister where the Benedictine monks whose monastery is attached to Saint Paul's come to meditate and pray.

The facade of the church includes many images. In the center pinnacle is Jesus, Saint Peter, and Saint Paul. Below are 12 lambs, symbolizing the apostles. Four Old Testament prophets reside under the image of the lambs. A Holy Door wishes those who enter peace and salvation.

Inside the church is one nave and four aisles. There are 80 columns. Images celebrate the life of Saint Paul. A special feature in the Basilica are medallions that honor each pope that can be found throughout the church. A legend says that when the remaining blank medallions in the Basilica are filled with images, the world will come to an end! A staircase leads below the church where visitors can see a large ancient sarcophagus that identifies the remains of "Paul, Apostle and Martyr." Carbon 14 testing of bone fragments confirm the bones are from the first or second century.

Holy Year of Mercy

On the second anniversary of Pope Francis's election to the Papacy, he announced an extraordinary Holy Year calling for a Jubilee of Mercy. This Holy Year of Mercy began on December 8, 2015, the Solemnity of the Immaculate Conception and the 50th Anniversary of the closing of Vatican II; it ended on November 20, 2016, the Solemnity of Our Lord Jesus Christ, King of the Universe.[24] Pope Francis wrote about the Jubilee Year of Mercy in his "Bull of Indiction of the Extraordinary Jubilee of Mercy."

---

[24] Joan Lewis, *A Holy year in Rome* (Manchester, NH: Sophia Institute Press, 2015) 85.

"May the Holy Spirit, who guides the steps of believers in cooperating with the work of salvation wrought by Christ, lead the way and support the People of God so that they may contemplate the face of mercy...How much I desire that the year to come will be steeped in mercy, so that we can go out to every man and woman, bringing the goodness and tenderness of God!"

Realizing that it is difficult if not impossible for many Catholics to go to Rome for pilgrimage, Pope Francis expanded the particulars of the Jubilee Year of Mercy for the indulgences associated with pilgrimages to the Papal Basilicas. To experience and obtain the Indulgence, the faithful were called to make a brief pilgrimage to enter through the Holy Door, open in every Cathedral or in the churches designated by the Diocesan Bishop, and in the four Papal Basilicas in Rome, as a sign of the deep desire for true conversion. Special considerations were also available to those who through illness or incarceration could not go to these designated sights. Indulgences were also received through the "faithful performance" of one of the Spiritual or Corporal Works of Mercy. Indulgences associated with Roman Pilgrimages were greatly expanded.

Pilgrim of Mercy and Music

A former Notre Dame football player is making his mark in the Holy Year of Mercy and beyond. Mike McGlinn was a Notre Dame University offensive tackle who played for Lou Holtz during the 1991-1994 seasons. He was an excellent player, but he had a more powerful pull from music and ministry than football. After graduation, he took his musical talents and performed with some top bands and musicians like

Gloria Estefan and the Miami Sound Machine, the Allman Brothers Band, and Genesis.

Mike is married with a family. He and his wife have three children and his mission in life is simply to help people become confident in God's goodness so that trust replaces fear, and love replaces worry. McGlinn has developed films, music, and productions that support his mission. McGlinn sings, plays piano, guitar, and bass. He reaches out to share his Catholic faith through film-making, music, speaking, and the arts. Mike believes that we have to take part in the heavy lifting of our lives and we should be "conversant with God."

In the Church's Year of Mercy, McGlinn set up a web site to support his efforts to promote Mercy and on the site he has short film clip reflections, music, and more.[25] McGlinn is a speaker with Catholic Athletes for Christ and he offers three presentations to parishes in which he mixes music and the arts that join in with community worship. As a former Notre Dame football player and a committed Christian, McGlinn has been a guest on Ron Meyer's Blessed2Play radio program.[26]

---

[25] See faceofmercy.com

[26] For the McGinn interview, go the Blessed2Play site at http://www.blessed2play.com/ and reference the interview on the show archives.

Morley Fraser: Let Him Show Mercy Cheerfully

Morley Fraser was the Chicago Bears' chapel speaker one Sunday, before the Bears played the Detroit Lions in Michigan. Fraser was a long time coach at Albion College in Albion, Michigan, and he had an inspirational message.

Both of my sons are football coaches and I was their chapel speaker this weekend. Ironically, the one yesterday was the underdog. He tried every trick I ever taught him. They warmed up on their own field which was five miles from the game field. A few injured players went out on the field for the coin toss.

PILGRIMAGE

Everyone was wondering whether the team was going to show up or not. They arrived just a few minutes before game time. After the game which was won 14-0, I had to wait along with the sportswriters while the team knelt in prayer.

Romans 12:6-13 is very important to me. "We have different gifts, according to the grace given us. If a man's gift is prophesying, let him use it in proportion to his faith. If it is serving, let him serve; if it is teaching, let him teach; if it is encouraging, let him encourage; if it is contributing to the needs of others, let him give generously; if it is leadership, let him govern diligently; if it is showing mercy, let him do it cheerfully.

"Love must be sincere. Hate what is evil; cling to what is good. Be devoted to one another in brotherly love. Honor one another above yourselves. Never be lacking in zeal, but keep your spiritual fervor, serving the Lord. Be joyful in hope, patient in affliction, faithful in prayer. Share with God's people who are in need. Practice hospitality."

Some players in the NFL don't put out. In Romans, the Lord said zeal and enthusiasm are very important. It has to be consistent. If you can't put out for 16 games, something is wrong.

If you take time out to enjoy things that God gave you for free, like sunrises and sunsets, you can be rejuvenated. There is no such thing as a flat game if the priorities are right.

If we make a mistake, we go to that person and apologize. Then go to God with courage and ask that you never harm that person again.

Patrick McCaskey

One of the jobs that you have is to beat the Lions. You also have the job of helping everyone else on the team and the staff. Everybody has to be ready for the game. Then take time with your family and get ready for the next game.

Church of the Visitation at Ein Karem

Chapter 4: Visitation

Many books have been written on the life of Mary, the Mother of God. We think of the great highs and lows in Mary's life. Many writers suggest that she had great enthusiasm for her life and the role she would play, but she must have had a sense of the sorrow to come. Regardless, Mary accepted God's plan and no doubt she was not someone who froze in her tracks overcome with anxiety. Mary acted—she took charge. And although she was pregnant herself, she packed her bags and went on a sacred journey, a pilgrimage that we call the Visitation. This was a special time for Mary and her actions speak volumes about her.

Mary was a young girl when she became engaged to Joseph. According to Luke 1:28-38, She was visited by the Angel Gabriel who greeted her with news:

"Hail, full of grace, the Lord is with you!"

But she was greatly troubled at the saying, and considered in her mind what sort of greeting this might be. And the angel said to her,

"Do not be afraid, Mary, for you have found favor with God. And behold, you will conceive in your womb and bear a son, and you shall call his name Jesus."

"He will be great, and will be called the Son of the Most High; and the Lord God will give to him the throne of his father David, and he will reign over the house of Jacob for ever; and of his kingdom there will be no end."

And Mary said to the angel,

"How can this be, since I have no husband?"

And the angel said to her,

"The Holy Spirit will come upon you, and the power of the Most High will overshadow you; therefore the child to be born will be called holy, the Son of God.

And behold, your kinswoman Elizabeth in her old age has also conceived a son; and this is the sixth month with her who was called barren. For with God nothing will be impossible."

And Mary said,

"Behold, I am the handmaid of the Lord; let it be to me according to your word." *And the angel departed from her."*

Mary became pregnant by the Holy Spirit with Jesus. When Joseph found out that Mary was pregnant, he was going to end the engagement the most humanitarian way possible, but according to Matthew 1:20-21, he was visited in a dream by an angel who told him:

"Joseph, son of David, do not fear to take Mary your wife, for that which is conceived in her is of the Holy Spirit; she will bear a son, and you shall call his name Jesus, for he will save his people from their sins."

Mary turned her attention towards her cousin Elizabeth. Elizabeth's husband Zechariah was visited by the Angel Gabriel while working in the temple. The angel told Zechariah that his wife Elizabeth will bear a son and his name shall be John who will *"make ready for the Lord a people prepared."*[27] When Zechariah questioned the angel because his wife was too old to bear children, his voice was taken away for the duration of Elizabeth's pregnancy.

Mary decided to help Elizabeth. We call her time with Elizabeth, the Visitation; it is remembered as the Second Joyful Mystery of the Rosary. Many people believe that Elizabeth lived in Ein Karem, on the western outskirts of Jerusalem. The trip from Nazareth could have taken about 10 days. It would have been a difficult trip for a young pregnant girl, but perhaps one of great joy for Mary whose future was filled with promise and purpose. It is likely that Joseph would have traveled with her and gone back home while she took care of her cousin. Regardless, the journey and her stay gives us a sense of just what a person Mary was and how her family faithfully looked after each other.

Mary's story continues in Luke 1:39-45:

---

[27] Luke 1:17

"In those days Mary arose and went with haste into the hill country, to a city of Judah, and she entered the house of Zechariah and greeted Elizabeth. And when Elizabeth heard the greeting of Mary, the babe leaped in her womb; and Elizabeth was filled with the Holy Spirit and she exclaimed with a loud cry, 'Blessed are you among women, and blessed is the fruit of your womb! And why is this granted me, that the mother of my Lord should come to me? For behold, when the voice of your greeting came to my ears, the babe in my womb leaped for joy. And blessed is she who believed that there would be a fulfilment of what was spoken to her from the Lord.'"

In Luke 1:46-55, Mary responds with her Song of Praise also called the Magnificat:

"My soul magnifies the Lord, and my spirit rejoices in God my Savior, for he has regarded the low estate of his handmaiden. For behold, henceforth all generations will call me blessed; for he who is mighty has done great things for me, and holy is his name. And his mercy is on those who fear him from generation to generation. He has shown strength with his arm, he has scattered the proud in the imagination of their hearts, he has put down the mighty from their thrones, and exalted those of low degree; he has filled the hungry with good things, and the rich he has sent empty away. He has helped his servant Israel, in remembrance of his mercy, as he spoke to our fathers, to Abraham and to his posterity forever."

When Mary and Elizabeth met up, it was one of the most memorable occasions in the Bible. Mary's visit is commemorated by the Visitation Church in Ein Karem. The Visitation would not be Mary's only holy journey.

Sister Miriam James

The Blessed Virgin Mary has an important role for the Sisters of the Society of Our Lady of the Most Holy Trinity (SOLT). Each sister makes her consecration to Jesus through Mary using the method given by Saint Louis de Montfort.[28]

Sister Miriam James Heidland was raised in Woodland, Washington, and attended the University of Nevada-Reno on a volleyball scholarship. After living a life of parties and fun at college, the Communications Major began to seek something more substantial and she turned to Jesus. She found a vocation with the Society of Our Lady of the Most Holy Trinity. Heidland has been determinedly working with elementary and high school students and athletes, co-hosting a radio program, and speaking to many different audiences around the country with SOLT.

Sister Miriam James talks much about what it means to be human and she says people today don't understand what it means. So many people "live like animals" because they don't understand this. She talks about how we can find sanctity. We can find excellence in our lives because Our Father is great.

Sister Miriam James is the author of *Loved as I Am: An Invitation to Conversion, Healing, and Freedom through Jesus.* Her book helps readers who hunger for a deeper relationship with God—it helps readers on the "great journey of authentic love."

According to Sister Miriam James, Jesus was secure because He knew who He was. We are made in the image of God—we are "very good" according to Genesis. But

---

[28] Saint Louis de Montfort was a French Priest with a strong devotion to Mary. He wrote several books that were popular with clergy and had a far-reaching impact on Catholics.

49

when Sister Miriam James was young she saw God as a policeman and thought she could be loved by God only if she was perfect. Sister Miriam James writes that we seek things that destroy us. Much of what she saw in herself was destructive. How could God love someone like her?

Sister Miriam James talks about her confusion when she found out that her parents adopted her. The moment her parents told her she was adopted, she found herself doubting God's plan. Sister Miriam James thought long about the deprivation that an infant might feel when they have no home. She came to accept that God does not believe a birth is an unintended circumstance. All births are special to God. We are not orphans, we are His children. Abortion, according to Sister Miriam, always leads to the death of a child, a unique individual that can never be recreated. When a child is aborted, we lose someone in our lives—a friend or relative; leader or spouse.

She found that each of us is someone who deserves to be loved rather than something that is used. All parts of us must be surrendered to God: spirit, soul, and body. Heidland writes about how each of us is planned, we are not unplanned or an accident.

We enter in communion with other people—"the intimacy we share with one another is a small spark of the intimacy God desires to have with us." Heidland writes that we need to let God find us. Freedom is being able to identify what is truly good and then choosing the good. Sister Miriam James is a great spokesperson for faith.

Notre Dame

We are lucky to have Jesus as our Guide and the example of the Blessed Virgin Mary. For the young, great examples of Christian faith can be found at schools coming from the people who guide those institutions and their patrons. I was blessed to have gone to Notre Dame of Niles. I am involved in events and organizations at the school.

Gentlemen of Mary

Unlike public schools with low tuition,
Where secular values go hand-in-hand;
Here at Notre Dame Character will stand
And sportsmanship will come to fruition.

Building and grounds are in fine condition.
Mary's gentlemen have improved the land.
It has taken more than a marching band.
The Moreau Mission is not sedition.
"As the Lord leads, we will go!" says Mary.
"Give me your boys, even the ones who foul,
Your boys yearning to breathe asbestos free,
The ones who will not throw in the towel.
We'll teach them and coach them for God's glory,
Discipline and awards without a scowl!"

—Patrick McCaskey

Chapter 5: Fatima

Portugal has a warm Mediterranean climate and a long history of exploration and colonialization that ended in the last half of the 20th century. It is also a Catholic country. When many think of Portugal, they think of Fatima and the apparitions that happened there. The year 2017 is the 100th Anniversary of the Marian Apparitions in Fatima.

In the spring and summer of 1916, 9-year-old Lúcia Santos and her cousins, Jacinta and Francisco Marto, were herding sheep at the Cova da Iria near their home village of Fátima. They were visited by an angel who taught them prayers and encouraged sacrifice. The angel appeared two more times. The following year, on May 13, 1917, Lúcia described seeing a lady "brighter than the sun..." Jacinta told her family about the apparition. Her mother told neighbors and they spread the news. Appearances on June 13 and July 13 occurred in which the lady asked the children to do penance and acts of reparation and make personal sacrifices to save sinners. Lúcia recounted that the lady gave the children three secrets, which have intrigued the public since.

Thousands of people came to Fátima to see the apparitions. On August 13, 1917, a local politician, Artur Santos, intercepted and jailed the children before they could reach the Cova da Iria. He threatened the children because they were causing a commotion. The children had their next apparition on August 15, the Feast of the Assumption, at nearby Valinhos. On October 13, 1917, what became known as the "Miracle of the Sun" occurred at Fatima. At Cova da Iria, a huge crowd stood with the children. Lúcia, seeing light rising from the lady's hands and the sun appearing as a silver disk, called out "look at the sun," as it changed colors and rotated. The children saw various images of Our Lady and the Holy Family that day.

In October 1930, after a canonical inquiry, the apparitions of Fátima were said to be "worthy of belief." Popes Pius XII (1939-1958), John XXIII (1958-1963), Paul VI (1963-1978), John Paul II (1978-2005), Benedict XVI (2005-2013), and Francis (2013-) have all supported the Fátima events. Most notably, Pope Saint John Paul II credited the intercession of Our Lady of Fatima for saving his life following an assassination attempt on the Feast of Our Lady of Fatima, 1981. The bullet from his wound was placed in the crown of the Virgin's statue.

Secrets

The first secret of Fatima was described by Lucia as a vision of hell: "Our Lady showed us a great sea of fire which seemed to be under the earth. Plunged in this fire were demons and souls in human form, like transparent burning embers, all blackened or burnished bronze"...

The second secret predicted a great sign in the night sky which would precede a second great war. Bright lights from the aurora borealis appeared just before Adolph Hitler seized Austria and eight months later invaded Czechoslovakia.

According to Joseph Cardinal Ratzinger, writing as the Prefect of the Congregation for the Doctrine of the Faith:

"For one terrible moment, the children were given a vision of hell. They saw the fall of "the souls of poor sinners". And now they are told why they have been exposed to this moment: "in order to save souls"—to show the way to salvation.

"To save souls" has emerged as the key word of the first and second parts of the "secret"...

The third secret is a vision of the death of religious figures. Our Lady and an Angel are looking down with a flaming sword—the Angel cries out, "Penance, Penance, Penance." A light suggested to Lucia the presence of God was also there. A number of religious figures including the Holy Father are climbing a mountain and at the top is a rough-hewn cross. According to Lucia, "the Holy Father passed through a big city half in ruins and half trembling with halting step, afflicted with pain and sorrow, he prayed for the souls of the corpses he met on his way; having reached the top of the mountain, on his knees at the foot of the big Cross he was killed by a group of soldiers who fired bullets and arrows at him, and in the same way there died one after another the other Bishops, Priests, Religious men and women, and various lay people of different ranks and positions. Beneath the two arms of the Cross there were two Angels each with a crystal aspersorium (holy water container) in which they gathered up the blood of the Martyrs and with it sprinkled the souls that were making their way to God."

The release of the third secret was made on June 26, 2000.

According to Cardinal Ratzinger:

... and the key word of this third part is the threefold cry: "Penance, Penance, Penance!" To understand the signs of the times means to accept the urgency of penance—of conversion–of faith. The angel with the flaming sword on the left of the Mother of God recalls similar images in the Book of Revelation. This represents the threat of judgement which looms over the world. Today the prospect that the world might be reduced to ashes by a sea of fire no longer seems pure fantasy: man himself, with his inventions, has forged the flaming sword. The vision then shows the power which stands opposed to the force of destruction—the splendour of the Mother of God and, stemming from this in a certain way, the summons to penance. In this way, the importance of human freedom is underlined: the future is not in fact unchangeably set, and the image which the children saw is in no way a film preview of a future in which nothing can be changed. Indeed, the whole point of the vision is to bring freedom onto the scene and to steer freedom in a positive direction. The purpose of the vision is not to show a film of an irrevocably fixed future. Its meaning is exactly the opposite: it is meant to mobilize the forces of change in the right direction...

Lúcia joined the Dorothean convent in Galicia in 1928. Francisco (1908–1919) and Jacinta Marto (1910–1920) died in the Great Spanish Flu Epidemic of 1918-20. Francisco and Jacinta were declared venerable by Pope Saint John Paul II in a public ceremony at Fátima on May 13, 1989 with Lucia present. The Pope returned there on May 13, 2000, also with Lucia, to declare them "blessed."

Sister Lúcia reported seeing the Virgin Mary again in 1925 and 1929 at the Dorothean convent in Galicia. Mary had requested the Consecration of Russia to her Immaculate Heart. Much has been written on this aspect of the apparitions and the relationship of them to Russia. In 1947, Sister Lúcia left the Dorothean order and joined the Discalced Carmelite Order in a monastery in Coimbra, Portugal. Lúcia died on February 13, 2005, at the age of 97.

Pope Pius XII in 1951 in his Apostolic Letter Sacro Vergente consecrated Russia to the Blessed Virgin Mary. Pope Pius XII and Pope Saint John Paul II were devoted to Our Lady of Fátima. Pope Pius XII was laid to rest in the crypt of Saint Peter's Basilica on October 13, 1958, the anniversary of the last apparition at Fátima. Pope Saint John Paul II consecrated the entire world to the Virgin Mary in 1984.

Angelo Giuseppe Roncalli, would become Pope Saint John XXIII and would famously open the Second Vatican Council. But the highly regarded Cardinal Roncalli, when he was Patriarch of Venice in 1956, spoke this prayer at the 25th Anniversary of the consecration of the country of Portugal to the Immaculate Heart of Mary:[29]

Bless all Europe, now more than ever tormented by profound divisions between those who think they can

---

[29] Pope John XXIII, *Pope John XXIII: Journal of a Soul* (New York: McGraw-Hill, 1964) 385.

build a new world without your son, the Saviour of the World, the Way, the Truth, and the Life, without remaining true to the traditions of their fathers.

Fatima draws thousands of pilgrims from around the world with its night-time processions. Pilgrims come to the Cova de Iria where the Virgin Mary appeared. On one side of the plaza rises the great basilica housing the tombs of Francisco and Jacinta Marto. Today the principal pilgrimage festivals take place on the anniversaries of the original appearances.

Kristin Holum—Sister Catherine Mary

Kristin Holum was a young speed skater with Olympic heritage and a big future. Like many skaters, she had started training very young—just before turning 7 years old. The sport is a natural for Kristin, she is the daughter of Diane Holum and Mike Devecka. Diane won a silver medal for the 500 meters and a bronze for the 1000 meters in the 1968 Olympics in Grenoble. She followed with the gold medal in the 1500 meter and the silver in the 3000 meters in Sapporo. Diane went on to coach both Eric Heiden, who won 5 Gold Medals in Lake Placid in 1980 and his sister Beth, who won a Bronze in Lake Placid as well. Kristin's father, skier Mike Devecka, competed in four different Olympic Winter Games: Grenoble, Sapporo, Innsbruck, and Lake Placid.

Training and sacrifice led Holum to top competitive form. At the same time, her mother provided a faith-based education at Catholic Schools. She went to Mass regularly and she knew Jesus deeply.

Working out 10 months a year, 6 days a week, several hours a day under her mother's guidance, she was at her best at 16 and won the World Junior All-Around Title.

Veteran skaters told her that she could be one of the best ever.

Encouraged by her mother, she broke from training to take a pilgrimage to Fatima—a life changing experience for her. When she walked into the Cova da Iria, the land that belonged to Lucia Santos's family where Mary appeared to the three children, she heard a voice say that she was going to be a religious sister. She went to the adoration chapel and sought more solace afterward. She added an extra prayer at her competitions, "Our Lady of Victory Pray for Me."

Competitive skating is never easy and it proved even more difficult for Holum as she was diagnosed with exercise-induced asthma that required a lot of medications carefully administered to avoid performing enhanced substance abuse problems. At age 17, she went on to the 1998 Olympics at Nagano, Japan, where she placed 6th in the 3000 meter and seventh in the 5000 meter. And although her sport was one where older athletes generally excel, she decided to go to college rather than continue to compete.

Holum attended the Art Institute of Chicago and studied photography. It was a far cry from her skating training and a long way from her religious experience at Fatima. "I didn't have any Christian friends, let alone any Catholic ones," she told the *National Catholic Register*. "So, by the time I graduated, I had completely forgotten about my call to be a sister. I moved to live with my mother after that, not knowing what the next step in my life would be."

In 2002, after finishing graduate school, Holum joined a pro-life walk across the United States and met Pope Saint John Paul II. She traveled with a devout group of young people who prayed the rosary and went to daily mass. This pilgrimage concluded in Toronto,

Canada, where World Youth Days were going on. She met the Franciscan Sisters of the Renewal, a religious order that helps the poor and homeless. She recalled the voice from Fatima. She went on to study. She took her final vows in 2010. Today, she is Sister Catherine Mary stationed in Leeds, England, at Saint Joseph's Convent. Her convent runs soup kitchens and distributes food.

In her work, when Sister Catherine Mary talks to young people about her vocation, they are moved by what she has accomplished and what she has embraced.

Red Bainbridge Volunteers

Red Bainbridge began his skating at the age of six. He competed in singles, pairs, and dance. He was an auxiliary member of the 1948 Olympic Team, a two time North American Dance Champion, a three time National Dance Champion, a National Silver Dance Champion, a National Junior Pairs Champion, and a National Junior Men's Silver medalist.

Bainbridge became an accomplished coach. His skaters obtained United States Figure Skating Association Gold Medals in figures, free style, and dance. They became National medal winners and took medals at the World Figure Skating Championships. He was named to the Washington Figure Skating Club's National and International Hall of Fame. He was inducted into the Professional Skaters Association Hall of Fame. The Buffalo Skating Club presents an annual Bainbridge Cup to beginner skaters in his honor who have demonstrated the most progress and enthusiasm for skating during the current season.

Red has generously volunteered for Church and charities. For 10 years Red served on the board and as volunteer executive director for Christian tapes for the blind and disabled. He has served on the board for numerous Pro-life organizations including Life Decisions International. He has volunteered for the Respect Life Office of the Catholic Diocese of Rockford for 10 years and presently serves Catholic Charities as a volunteer Ombudsman for long Term Care. For over 60 years, Bainbridge has been a professional skating coach, national and international medalist, instructor, judge, and charitable volunteer. He was inducted into the Sports Faith International Hall of Fame.

Chapter 6: Lourdes

Lourdes is located in southern France in the foothills of the Pyrenees Mountains. Its climate is mild with a good amount of rain. Charlemagne fought the Moors over the area in the eighth century.[30] Throughout the centuries many battled over that part of France, but in 1844, Lourdes was a quiet town. That year a special child was born there named Marie-Bernarde Soubirous. After the Virgin Mary appeared to "Bernadette" 18 times, little would remain the same. Marian Apparitions made Lourdes one of the most popular places of Christian pilgrimage where millions of pilgrims visit.

---

[30] Charlemagne (742-814) or Charles the Great was a medieval emperor and king of the Franks who ruled a large part of Europe and converted his subjects to Christianity.

PILGRIMAGE

On February 11, 1858, young Bernadette went to gather firewood with her sister and another companion. When Bernadette stopped before crossing a small stream that the others had passed, she heard the sound of the wind. In the Massabielle Grotto nearby she saw a bright light. A beautiful young lady appeared to Bernadette. She did not identify herself, but after her visit, she beckoned Bernadette to return. On a later visit, the lady referred to herself as the "Immaculate Conception," a term for the Blessed Mother that was only penned 4 years earlier in 1854 in an official church document by Pope Pius IX (1846-1878). The Immaculate Conception of Mary is often confused by many as the conception of Christ through the action of the Holy Spirit in the Blessed Virgin Mary. But, the Immaculate Conception refers to the Blessed Virgin Mary being free from original sin at her conception in the womb of her mother, Saint Anne.

.. We declare, pronounce and define that the doctrine which asserts that the Blessed Virgin Mary, from the first moment of her conception, by a singular grace and privilege of almighty God, and in view of the merits of Jesus Christ, Saviour of the human race, was preserved free from every stain of original sin is a doctrine revealed by God and, for this reason, must be firmly and constantly believed by all the faithful.

Pope Pius IX, Ineffabilis Deus (1854)

Bernadette had no understanding of the term. She reported the vision to her parish priest, who was skeptical at first, but became convinced of her honesty when he considered Bernadette's limited exposure to anything remotely complex concerning the faith.

Before Bernadette was visited by the Lady, the area where the apparitions were to occur, had been a place where animals came to graze. The Lady instructed Bernadette to dig at a certain spot and to drink the water that would bubble up. The spring that was uncovered was clear and clean. In the later appearances, the Lady asked for a chapel to be built. Discussions between Bernadette and the Lady were about prayer and penance. During the apparitions, Bernadette prayed the Rosary.

After the apparitions became known, cures were reported from those drinking the water, which has become the focus for many pilgrims to the Shrine at Lourdes. Today people bathe in the water.

Bernadette was the eldest of 9 children and her family had fallen on hard times. The family lived in one-room in a house owned by relative. Their quarters had once been used as a jail. It could not have been healthy for Bernadette who was a sickly child.

"Worthy of Belief"

Church authorities confirmed the authenticity of the apparitions; they were said to be "worthy of belief" in 1862. An estimated 200 million people have visited the shrine and the Catholic Church recognizes 69 healings considered miraculous. Healings are rigorously investigated for authenticity.

Bernadette went to a school run by the Sisters of Charity and in 1866, she and other candidates took the religious habit of a postulant and joined the Sisters of Charity at their motherhouse at Nevers. She was given the name Sister Marie-Bernarde. She worked humbly in the convent in the infirmary and later as a sacristan. She created beautiful altar cloths and vestments. For Sister Marie-Bernarde, she had done what Our Lady had asked her and she wanted no further attention from the masses of people turning out at Lourdes. Sister Marie-Bernarde would live to be 35 years old. She was buried at Saint Gildard Convent. Sister Marie-Bernarde, Saint Bernadette, was canonized a saint by Pope Pius XI (1922-1939) on December 8, 1933. Today, inside a chapel at the church of Saint Gildard, Saint Bernadette lies in a glass coffin.

As Sister Marie-Bernarde worked in the convent, Lourdes was developing as a pilgrimage site. The Basilica of the Immaculate Conception was finished there in 1871. The Pilgrimage to Lourdes is so popular, the area has many hotels, some say second only to Paris in France.

The film "Song of Bernadette" based on a book by Franz Werfel depicts the Lourdes story and apparitions. It won four Academy Awards in 1944.

Congregation of Holy Cross

From humble beginnings in France, Saint Bernadette's faith has had a great influence on a world-wide audience that loves the Blessed Virgin Mary. Others from France have been influential as well.

Born Basile-Antoine Marie Moreau in Laigné-en-Belin, in the Diocese of Le Mans, France, on February 11, 1799, Moreau was affected by the spiritual upheaval of the French Revolution. Church property was seized, priests were executed, and religious communities were expelled.

In 1821, Moreau was ordained a priest for the diocese, later becoming a seminary professor, teaching philosophy and theology. He organized a group of young priests who traveled the diocese, assisting in education and spiritual growth. Bishop Jean-Baptiste Bouvier of the Le Mans Diocese asked him to oversee the Brothers of Saint Joseph, a group that he merged with priests under a new order, the "Congregation of Holy Cross." [31]

The Cross became an integral part of his community's spirituality. Its motto is Ave Crux, Spes Unica ("Hail the Cross, Our Only Hope"). Blessed Moreau's vision was to maximize the spiritual vigor of his order to give it "one heart, one soul," by modeling it after the Holy Family and adding a group of sisters for education and evangelization.

Moreau started sending members to other countries, including Algeria, Canada, Bangladesh, and the United States. He sent seven young men, six brothers and Rev. Edward Sorin to the United States, where in 1842, they founded the University of Notre Dame. In 1857, the Holy

---

[31] Bouvier published a multivolume series on theology that would be used in seminaries around the world called *Institutiones Theologicæ*.

See officially declared Moreau's group to be a religious congregation and the Congregation of Holy Cross was born. Moreau died on Jan. 20, 1873, and he was beatified on Sept. 15, 2007.

Haley Scott

Life gives us trials that we do not expect. Often, those who are around us, with support from God, help us make it through. When we are part of a Christian community, we are never alone.

It's January 24, 1992, Haley Scott is a freshman on Notre Dame's Swim Team. Haley and her teammates are on the team bus on the Indiana Tollway approaching South Bend, Indiana. They are heading home after a meet at Northwestern University in Evanston, Illinois. It's snowing and the weather is blustery. The driver changes lanes to pass a car. The bus hits a patch of black ice as it moves back into the right lane, the bus slides off the road, fishtails, and then hits a culvert and flips over. Athletes are bounced around the vehicle, some windows are dislodged. Two team members, Meghan Beeler and Coleen Hipp, are expelled from the bus and crushed when it lands on them. It is just a few miles from the Notre Dame campus in the early morning hours and wreckage is scattered all around. Of the remaining injured, Haley Scott lies in the snow, seriously injured. She knows nothing of her two friends who are dead a short distance from her. She is alone for a few seconds. She feels nothing below the waist. Teammates begin to walk around and take care of the injured.

Rushed to a hospital, Scott undergoes two emergency surgeries that give her hope of recovery. Some hospital staff believe Scott will be paralyzed for the rest of her life, but she does not believe them. Her parents, Stephen and Charlotte Scott; siblings, Stephen Jr. and Mary Frances Scott; staff; friends; and many people at the University focus on her well-being. Notre Dame President Father Edward Malloy drops by and prays with Scott—an event that she would later remember as life-changing.

Notre Dame Athletic Director, Dick Rosenthal; Swim Team Coach, Tim Welsh; teachers; friends; swim team members; and even the Glee Club come to encourage Scott any way they can. It seems everyone at the school has embraced Haley Scott for the duration of her recovery. The following day, she learns of her teammates' deaths.

Students pray at the Notre Dame Grotto of Our Lady of Lourdes, designed after the famed French shrine where the Virgin Mary appeared to Saint Bernadette. Prayers are also said at the hospital, at the school chapel, and in dorm rooms on campus. Prayers are said for the deceased athletes and for Scott and other injured teammates. Scott's siblings and parents are committed to see her return to complete health no matter how discouraged things become. Scott herself dedicates the effort she makes to honor her two friends who died in the crash. She receives encouragement from their parents.

Challenges Continue

The rods that help hold Scott's spine together have started to detach months after her original surgeries. She goes to a specialist in San Diego, Dr. Garfin, for a difficult and dangerous procedure to replace the rods and straighten her spine. After a long surgery, she suffers from yet additional problems: a torn lymph duct, congestive heart failure, a collapsed lung, and her spine is not straightened. Physically spent by the procedures, she undergoes another surgery to fix the lymph duct problem and her surgeon decides to try one more time to straighten out her spine. Miraculously, the surgery is successful and her spine is straightened. Months of recovery follow. Friends, relatives, teachers, and administrators at Notre Dame continue to support Scott in every way possible. Wherever she goes, a steady stream of visitors follow.

Scott returns to the swim team and she wins a 50 Yard freestyle race upon her return. It's the highpoint of her swimming career and symbol of her recovery. It's a symbol for Notre Dame as well—the school named after Our Lady musters the faith of their students, teachers, and administrators to overcome discouragement and tragedy.

After School

Haley Scott graduated from Notre Dame and taught history and coached swimming at Xavier College Preparatory in Phoenix. Later, she married Jamie DeMaria, former ND Swim Team Manager. The couple has two sons and live in Annapolis, Maryland.

Haley Scott DeMaria wrote a book about her life called *What Though the Odds* published by Cross Training Publishing in 2008. She received many awards including the Spirit of Notre Dame Award, the *Executive*

Journal Comeback of the Year Award, the Honda Award for Inspiration, the Gene Autry Courage in Sport Award, and the Sports Faith International Virtues of Saint Paul Award, among others. She was named Woman of the Year at the National Women's Leadership Conference in Washington, DC and a Fellow at the Institute for International Sport in Rhode Island. Haley was involved in several Christian churches. After her many years of Catholic Education including her college career at Notre Dame, Scott became a Catholic. Today, she is an inspirational speaker.

Cathedral High School

Cathedral High School is a Catholic college preparatory school in Indianapolis that operates in the Holy Cross tradition. Opportunities for spiritual, intellectual, social, emotional, and physical growth through service and academic excellence are provided. Part of the Indianapolis community since 1918, Cathedral passes on the values and philosophy of educating the whole child, heart, mind, and spirit in an atmosphere of inclusion and diversity.

Cathedral's alumni athletes have earned medals in the Olympics and several play or have played in the National Football League and Major League Baseball. Cathedral alums also include the Indianapolis mayor, Gregory A. Ballard, and Tanya Marie Walton Pratt, the first African American federal judge in Indiana's history.

Cathedral's Lady Irish Volleyball Team were inducted into the Sports Faith International All Star Catholic Hall of Fame in 2009 for their accomplishments both on and off the court. The team is coached by former Ball State University All-American Jean Kesterson who has amassed more than 800 wins and seven State

Championships. In Community Service, both the athletes and coaches excel. They fuel their efforts with spiritual exercises including Mass on Friday mornings and prayer at games.

Christiana Gray Honors God

Exceptional schools help develop exceptional people. In 2009, Christiana Gray was inducted into the Catholic High School Hall of Fame as Athlete of the Year. Gray was an exceptional Volleyball player for Cathedral High School's Lady Irish, ranked fourth in the country.

Gray carried a 4.27 GPA in addition to her numerous extracurricular activities. Christiana or T as she is nicknamed, stands 6-feet-5 ½. Despite her intimidating figure at the net and feisty spirit, T stands tall in her virtue and love of God. She says God made her tall and we should be proud of everything God creates. She advises her younger peers to "walk tall, walk proud, and always wear heels."

Gray was chosen to the Indiana High School Athletic Association Role Model Program, appearing on posters throughout the state promoting sportsmanship. After graduating from Cathedral, Gray went on to Duke University and was named All-ACC three seasons, named All-ACC Academic Team, and was on the ACC Academic Honor Roll. She led Duke in many categories and she finished her career with 1,112 kills, which ranked 18th on the school career list. Her .350 career hitting percentage ranked third at Duke and eighth all-time in the ACC. She totaled 491 career blocks, a mark which ranked fourth in Duke History, and averaged 1.03 blocks per set to sit in seventh place in the school records.

In spite of all this recognition, her Cathedral High School Coach Jean Kesterson said: "I have never had a more humble, team-like player than Christiana. She works so hard in practice because she feels she has a responsibility to all involved and that she needs to honor God by using all her gifts. As phenomenal a player as she is, Christiana is a much better person."

Today, Christiana (Gray) Hill specializes in helping tall women manage their inner critic and cultivate confidence by leveraging her unique athletic & health coaching background.[32]

Chase Hilgenbrinck: Lord What Do You Want?

Mount Saint Mary's Seminary in Emmitsburg is the home of the National Shrine Grotto of Our Lady of Lourdes. This shrine features one of the oldest American replicas of the Lourdes shrine. It was built about two decades after the apparitions of Mary at Lourdes in 1858. It attracts hundreds of thousands of pilgrims each year from all over the world.

Chase Hilgenbrinck was a former professional soccer player and he left the game to study for the priesthood at Mount Saint Mary's Seminary. His vocation came as a surprise to the athlete. His parents, Mike and Kim, raised their children in the Catholic Church—attended Mass every Sunday. Both of their sons, Chase and Blaze served as altar boys at Holy Trinity Catholic Church in Bloomington, Illinois. Chase Hilgenbrinck had ambitions like many young boys to become a professional athlete.

---

[32] See Hill's site at: http://www.christianahill.com/

PILGRIMAGE

Hilgenbrinck made the United States Under-17 national soccer team, before moving on to play for Clemson University. While at Clemson, Hilgenbrinck was a 4-year starter, helping the Tigers to the 2001 ACC Championship and four NCAA tournament berths, including two Elite Eight appearances.

After graduating from Clemson in 2004 with a Bachelor's degree in Spanish and International Trade, Hilgenbrinck moved all the way down to Chile to follow his dream. He signed with Club Deportivo Huachipato of the Chilean First Division and was loaned out to a second-division club, Deportes Naval. In 2006, Chase moved on to popular Nublense, and helped the team achieve promotion to Chile's top division. The 2007 season was Hilgenbrinck's fourth and final in the Chilean league. Two of those years, he was selected as the best player at the left fullback position in the league.

Hilgenbrinck's success in soccer failed to satisfy him. He asked the Lord: "What is it that you are asking me to do that will bring me comfort and bring me peace?" The answer he got back: "be my priest." It was something that he did not want to hear. And yet, being a professional athlete and trying to live according to his faith was difficult. He went to church regardless of where he was and it helped make him feel at home.

Hilgenbrinck moved back to the United States in early 2008. He joined the Colorado Rapids, but was waived to clear salary cap space. Two weeks later, on March 28, Chase signed a new contract with the New England Revolution. On July 13, 2008, after three months with the team, Hilgenbrinck suited up for his last professional game when the Revolution faced Mexican club, Santos Laguna, at Gillette Stadium in Foxborough, Massachusetts.

Hilgenbrinck retired from soccer on July 14, 2008 to enter Mount Saint Mary's Seminary in hopes of becoming a Catholic priest. He had finally responded to God's call: "I trust you enough to say yes to this." Doing what God has asked him to do makes him happy. He described his seminary life as an especially happy time for him. He became the Head Sports Chaplain at the school.

Hilgenbrinck received the Sports Faith International Father Smyth Award. The Award honors an athlete who pursues a religious vocation. Hilgenbrinck was ordained a priest for the Diocese of Peoria on May 24, 2014.

Our Lady of Lourdes Parish

Our Lady of Lourdes Parish on Ashland Avenue in Chicago was established in 1892 just 30 years after the Marian Apparitions at Lourdes received the Church's "Worthy of Belief" confirmation. One of the ministries the parish offers is its "soup kitchen" that has run continuously since 1980. Home cooked meals are provided, never soup, and the 300 weekly guests leave with a sack lunch.

The Pastor, Father Michael Shanahan, is from the South Side of Chicago and a graduate of Brother Rice High School. He is a musician and he has a special passion for the needs of immigrants.[33] Father Shanahan says the parishioners of Our Lady of Lourdes "have come from many corners of the world and from different ways

---

33 Delores Madlener, "A Little Book and a Huge Crisis Reorganized His World," 5 Minutes with Father, *Catholic New World*, January 6-9, 2013. Viewed   at http://www.catholicnewworld.com/cnwonline/2013/0106/5min.aspx on June 8, 2016.

of life. Thousands of families and individuals have known the face of God as a result of their kindness."

Father Shanahan asked me to speak to parishioners and guests one evening in 2016 after their soup kitchen meal. I talked about my Catholic roots, my faith, my family, and my team to this great audience.

Saint Bernadette once described her calling as "I will spend every moment loving." Certainly that's a prevailing principle at Our Lady of Lourdes.

Football Autism Camp at Xavier High School

Writer Edna Ferber and Magician Harry Houdini spent some of their formative years in Appleton, Wisconsin. The city is 30 miles southwest of Green Bay in an area famous for paper-making. Appleton features 24 parks and produces the 4-day Mile of Music Festival. Lawrence University calls Appleton home as does Xavier High School.

Xavier High School prepares students to be leaders in the community and in the Church. Xavier is recognized as one of the top 50 Catholic high schools in the nation and a School of Distinction by the Diocese of Green Bay.

The Xavier Football Team supports children with autism. Football Autism Camp is one of the school's community services programs. Many children with Autism find social interactions difficult—typical communication and contact with others can be particularly challenging. Children may not understand how to play with other children and may prefer to be by themselves. Xavier Team members and coaches complete an education program to help them conduct the camp.

The children arrive at camp and under the leadership of Coach Dave Hinkens and his staff, twelve different stations are manned by team members to teach the basics of playing football. The children put on football equipment (if they choose). At the end of the day, campers score a touchdown and the cheerleaders cheer for them. All receive commemorative medals and run through a tunnel of football players, all giving them high fives.

Xavier athletes report that the Autism Football Camp is the best day of football—better than any big win because they feel they have made a difference in the life of a child. Accolades for the coach, the team, and the school were received by the Autism Society of Fox Valley, among others.

In addition to the Autism Camp, key to the team success is a three day lock-in retreat that is held at the beginning of the season for all the players and coaches. They perform team building activities, set goals, and pray together. Families are invited one night for Mass and dinner.

The team plays their home games on the Rocky Bleier Field named after the Pittsburgh Steelers running back who attended Xavier High School. Bleier recovered from devastating wounds suffered in Viet Nam to have a remarkable career.

Xavier football chaplain, Father Quinn Mann, attends to their spiritual direction. The Xavier Football Team received the Light of Christ Award from Sports Faith International.

Chapter 7: Assisi Pilgrimage

Assisi is an important pilgrimage site in Italy. Both Saint Francis and Saint Clare are buried in Assisi. Saint Francis is buried in the Basilica of San Francesco and Saint Clare in the Basilica of Santa Chiara. In Santa Chiara, people pray in front of a special crucifix of great importance to Saint Francis's life, which was originally at San Damiano. San Damiano is where Saint Clare's community lived. Many join the Friars who now live in San Damiano in prayer. Vespers, the evening service, is especially well-attended. There are many holy places for people to see when making a pilgrimage to Assisi.

Saint Francis

Saint Francis was born in Assisi in 1182, the son of a wealthy cloth merchant, Pietro Bernardone, and his wife, Pica. Francis enjoyed a busy social life. He wanted to be a knight. It was not his calling. In a local battle, he was captured and his father paid a ransom for his return. Afterward, Saint Francis experienced a serious illness. After his recovery, he set out on another military quest and got sick again. He went on a pilgrimage to Rome and experienced a tug to seek faith and abandon wealth.

The San Damiano Cross depicted the passion, death, and resurrection of Christ—the entire Paschal Mystery. Francis was drawn to the cross when he heard a voice call out three times: "Francis go and repair my house which you see is falling down."[34] Francis took the order literally and he began to rebuild churches. He quickly ran out of money and took cloth from his father's shop and sold it. His father was so upset with the young man that he disowned him. In a dramatic scene, Francis makes reparations to his father and strips off his clothes, returning to his father everything he had received from him.

Francis was strictly devoted to a new life of poverty and lived simply. Others followed and in time, he was building up a great following and an order that was called the Friars Minor. Francis wrote a Rule for his brothers in 1209 that was approved by the Church. He wrote a longer one in 1223, which has continued to shape the lives of the

---

[34] There are many biographies of Saint Francis. *Butler's Lives of the Saints* in many editions includes this story.

Franciscan Brothers. Saint Francis spent his life preaching with periods of prayer and solitude. He continued a humble life and many people were impressed by it. He received the Stigmata–the marks of the crucified Christ on his own body. He died in 1226, and he was quickly declared a saint in 1228.

In many ways, Saint Francis did help rebuild the Church. The Franciscans *"give their lives to the Gospel of Jesus Christ in humble and compassionate service with special concern for the poor and marginalized."*[35]

Saint Clare

Saint Clare was born in 1194, the daughter of a nobleman in Assisi. She shared her food with the poor. She was captivated by Saint Francis's preaching. On Palm Sunday 1212, she left her parents' house and at Saint Mary of the Angels Church near Assisi, she met Saint Francis and she took a simple habit. Saint Francis cut her hair. She made a vow of obedience to Saint Francis and she lived with a Benedictine community of nuns. Her sister, Agnes, joined her soon afterward. Her family failed in attempts to have her returned to them.

When Clare and Agnes moved to San Damiano, the first community of Poor Clares came into being. In 1215, Clare was made Abbess, a position she held until her death in 1253. She was declared a saint in 1255. Her sister Agnes became Abbess as well. Agnes was declared a saint in 1753.

---

[35] Mission statement of the Franciscan Friars of Santa Barbara at https://www.sbfranciscans.org/about.

Patrick McCaskey

Sister Rita Clare Yoches

On August 23, 2012, a news item appeared in the *Michigan Catholic*, the official publication of the Archdiocese of Detroit:

... Sister Rita Clare Yoches, the daughter of Robert and Mary Yoches of Saint Frances Cabrini Parish, Allen Park, made her first profession of vows of poverty, chastity and obedience with the Franciscan Sisters, T.O.R. (Third Order Regular) of Penance of the Sorrowful Mother, on Aug. 6 before Bishop Emeritus Gilbert Sheldon of the Diocese of Steubenville, Ohio.

The story was expressed plainly, but those who have met Sister Rita Clare, know the Franciscans have a great energetic and lively new Sister.[36]

---

[36] Conversion story can be found at Franciscan Sisters T.O.R. of Penance of the Sorrowful Mother at http://www.franciscansisterstor.org/about-us/meet-the-sisters/sister-rita-clare/ and you can listen to an interview

Yoches attended Catholic grade school and high school in Dearborn, Michigan. Her family attended Mass every Sunday and for her that was much of what being Catholic was all about. Super athletic Yoches, who was often coached by her dad, played volleyball, soccer, softball, golf, and basketball at Divine Child High School and she had little time for faith. She continued to succeed at sports and received a full scholarship to play Division I basketball at the University of Detroit-Mercy. She started all 4 years and captained the last 2.

She graduated with a degree in sports medicine. While in college, like many students, she lost track of what would become her top priority, her faith.

After graduation, she worked as a strength and conditioning coach at Notre Dame University. She played women's professional football with the South Bend Golden Hawks and then the Detroit Demolition where her team won four National Championships. But mixed into her sports career was a continuing battle with evil—a little too much party. One Sunday at Mass, she reflected on the Priest's sermon on 1 Corinthians 11:27-30:

Whoever, therefore, eats the bread or drinks the cup of the Lord in an unworthy manner will be guilty of profaning the body and blood of the Lord. Let a man examine himself, and so eat of the bread and drink of the cup. For anyone who eats and drinks without discerning the body eats and drinks judgment upon himself. That is why many of you are weak and ill, and some have died.

Yoches saw the detour she had taken, she got the message, and she acted quickly. She went to Confession

---

of Sister Rita Clare Yoches at http://www.blessed2play.com/show-archives/page/2.

and she began to reform her life and renew her faith. She listened to Catholic radio, read the Bible, and went to Eucharistic Adoration.

On a pilgrimage with her mother to Assisi, Italy, in 2004 Yoches first began hearing the call to religious life: *I was outside of Saint Clare's Basilica after praying in front of the San Damiano Cross. I was watching the Poor Clares walk inside the church when I heard the Lord say to me in my heart, "You should do this, you could do this." I said, "Do what!?!?! You've got to be kidding me, do you know who I am and what I have done in my life? Plus I don't even know anyone who still does that." I just pretended that nothing happened and I did not tell anyone, but it would not go away. Every night there was a whisper in my heart saying you have a calling. Six months later I went to a discernment retreat just to check it off my list and make sure religious life was not for me. I liked it but was not ready to surrender my life just yet.*

Yoches went to visit a convent and had a vision of religious life. Later she told herself that she would seek a religious vocation, but she met a great Catholic guy. Again, she wrestled with her future. At two different Festivals of Praise a year apart at Franciscan University of Steubenville, people prayed over her—the first time she received a confirmation of her vocation although she was still not ready—the second time she received a kind of cleansing that helped her know that the Lord was welcoming her regardless of her past sins. As others prayed over her the second time, she kneeled, wept, and eventually fell prostrate to the ground. When she got up, she saw the big San Damiano Cross hanging in the fieldhouse—"The Lord had brought me full circle from the first time He called me in Assisi to now," she thought.

About a month later, she felt like she was finally becoming the "person Christ intended me to be, the person I always wanted to be."

Matthew Anzalone for Life

Matthew Anzalone is one of eight children. Home schooled through grade eight, Matthew transitioned well to the public high school system. He achieved academic honors all 4 years. On the Lemont High School football team, he started on the defensive line for 3 years and was team captain for 2 of those. In 2008, an undefeated Lemont High School at 13-0 advanced to the 6A State Championship game where they lost to Sacred Heart-Griffin.[37] Matthew's 53 tackles, 4 sacks, and 4 fumble recoveries earned him numerous awards.

Off the field, in his "American Problems" Class, Matthew often spoke out in defense of life. While still in high school, he demonstrated for life in front of Planned Parenthood and was a volunteer at a women's crisis and pregnancy center. Twice, he participated in the Annual March for Life in Washington, DC. Add to this his visitations to nursing homes, distribution of food to the poor on a bread-truck in Chicago, and his participation in a Catholic Heart Work Mission Camp in Louisville, Kentucky, and you will understand why he received the Sports Faith International Prayers for Life National Apostolate Award.

---

[37] Sacred Heart Griffin is a football powerhouse in Illinois and their involvement in the 2013 Washington tornado relief effort is found in our book, Patrick McCaskey's, *Sports and Faith: More Stories of the Devoted and the Devout* (Crystal Lake, IL, Sporting Chance Press, 2015) 1-5.

Patrick McCaskey

Two Rassas Brothers

What do "The Star Spangled Banner" and Nick Rassas have in common? *They were born in Baltimore.*

Nick played football for Loyola Academy. Then he was a walk-on at the University of Notre Dame.

From Jim Dent's book, *Resurrection: The Miracle Season That Saved Notre Dame*, we know that, "the walk-on worked as hard as anyone on the team. He gained weight, maintained a cheery disposition, sang the 'Victory March' at every pep rally, and kept his grade-point average above a 3.0. But he was never promoted past the fifth string."

Fortunately, a junior varsity scrimmage was filmed when Nick played very well. "He broke several long runs from the halfback position, and returned two punts for touchdowns. He also intercepted two passes and returned one for a touchdown."

In the final game of the 1963 season, Nick started. In 1964, he started. In 1965, he was an All-American. He was a second round draft choice of the Atlanta Falcons. He played in the 1966 College All Star Game. He played for the Falcons from 1966 through 1968. He played very well against the Chicago Bears. Before every one of his games, "The Star Spangled Banner" was sung.

Nick's brother, Bishop Rassas, says that Nick is very humble about his accomplishments. When Nick was coaching football at Loyola Academy, he told the players that the movie "Rudy" should have been about him.

Now Nick is a Sports Faith International Hall of Famer.

Bishop George Rassas was born in Baltimore. He grew up in Winnetka; he was an excellent altar boy for Faith, Hope, and Charity Church.

When he was the pastor of Saint Mary's Lake Forest, I was one of his lectors. Before one Easter Sunday morning Mass, I said to him, "There's a huge crowd. I guess they heard that I was the lector."

He replied, "You solved the mystery."

At the end of another Mass, he said to the congregation, "Please feel free to take any lady bugs with you."

After he became the vicar general of the Archdiocese of Chicago, he recommended that Father Michael McGovern succeed him as pastor of Saint Mary's. He said, "That was the only time that Cardinal George listened to me."

After he became a bishop, my son, Jim, and Tommy Rees were in his Confirmation class. Then Tommy threw many touchdown passes for the University of Notre Dame.

Sports Faith International has a Catholic radio station, WSFI, 88.5 FM. The tower is in Antioch; the studio is in Libertyville, right down the hall from Bishop Rassas. He is an excellent neighbor.

Bishop Rassas is an eminent eminence. His vicariate is a halfway house to heaven. He is representing Christ the King.

My Faith Based Education

People may be surprised today to find that many professional sports families are not only Catholic, but products of Catholic education. When my grandfather, George "Papa Bear" Halas, ran the Chicago Bears, he competed with several Catholic owners and coaches. Wellington Mara of the New York Giants, Art Rooney of the Pittsburgh Steelers, and Coach Vince Lombardi of the Green Bay Packers come to mind. On the football field, things were strictly business between these men, but off the field these men were all practicing Catholics who would occasionally break bread together.

My mother, Virginia McCaskey, daughter of Papa Bear, married my father, Edward McCaskey, of Lancaster, Pennsylvania. My father came to Chicago because he loved my mother. He left a great deal behind in Lancaster where his family of soldiers, musicians, and educators had established themselves. My parents had a large family of 11 children. They sent all of us to Catholic Grade Schools and High Schools. Some attended Catholic colleges as well.

I was baptized at Saint Mary's Church in Des Plaines, Illinois. My aunt, Flossie McCaskey, was my godmother. Her son, Pat, was killed during World War II. My grandfather, George Halas, was my godfather.

When I was in second grade at Saint Mary's School, I was in Sister Amata's class. I was in the Bluebirds reading group. I used to enjoy getting up in front of the class and reading to them. Now I'm a lector at Saint Mary's Church in Lake Forest.

The teachers encouraged the students to be positive role models. We were usually seated in alphabetical order. There were times when misbehaving students were seated next to students who behaved. Don Nevins often sat next to me. He is now an excellent priest.

On my eighth birthday, I went to school in the morning. Sister Amata announced to the class that my father was taking me out of school in the afternoon. He was taking me to see the movie "Around the World in Eighty Days" at the Michael Todd Theater in Chicago.

When the Saint Mary's second graders made their First Confessions, I said, "Bless me Father for I have sinned. Three days ago I played hooky." I asked for penance and absolution.

A couple days later, the Saint Mary's second graders made their First Communions. Two years later, we received the Sacrament of Confirmation. My grandfather, Dick McCaskey, was my sponsor. My Confirmation name was Paul. I liked the apostle Paul. He wrote a lot of letters even though the Corinthians were the only ones who ever wrote back.

After Mass on First Fridays, we were allowed to stand at tables in the school hall and eat breakfast with hot chocolate that cost 10 cents a cup. The proceeds went to the missions.

We were also allowed to buy candy at lunchtime in that hall. The proceeds went to the missions. We saw many excellent movies in that hall for 10 cents that went to the missions. We saw "The Bells of Saint Mary's," "The Glenn Miller Story," "Pride of the Yankees," "The Spirit of Saint Louis," and "The Student Prince."

When I was in seventh grade, I started at forward on the eighth grade basketball team. We had one victory. Saint Joseph the Worker got way ahead and put in their second string. Before they could recover, we won 14–12. We lost to Saint James 46–1. I led the team in scoring.

When I was in eighth grade, the basketball team was very successful. We won the Maryville Academy Don Bosco Tournament at the end of the season. Then we had an eighth grade assembly in the school hall. When I presented the trophy to Father Bird, he asked me, "What do you want me to do with it?" I'm glad that he didn't give it to the missions.

My Catholic school experiences and friendships have followed me through life. When I got married and when my sons were baptized, my Saint Mary's classmate, Father Nevins, was the priest. When it was time for Saint

Mary's 25-year class reunion, Father Nevins provided the homily that turned out to be the highlight of the occasion.

He was tempted to talk exclusively about things that happened 25 years ago, but he did not yield. He urged the congregation to look forward with something in common. He pointed out that we grew up in the same classrooms and in the same community. He reminded us that the kind of education that we received was worthwhile.

Father Nevins cited George Gallop's poll of the contribution of Catholic education.

First, Catholic education had great quality. It was always first class. It offered a great deal to the community. Second, Catholic education lifts people up to a future that can lift the next generation up. People obtain a sense of self-esteem and confidence. Third, because of the size of Catholic education, it created a sense of community, the meaning of life itself. Fourth, Catholic education focused on values that are focused on Jesus. Values have to be passed on from one generation to another. Jesus shared His Life with His Apostles. That life brought the people together as one. As we come together, we ask all of you to pass on the values. People who hear the word of the Lord should share it with one another.

Letter from Uncle Mugs

Because of eye and allergy problems, it took me six years to complete my undergraduate class work. Then it took me another two years to finish some term papers and a correspondence course. On December 13, 1976, the Dean of the College of Arts and Sciences at Indiana University sent me a form letter.

PILGRIMAGE

Dear Mr. McCaskey:

The Recorder of the College of Arts and Sciences has informed me that you have now completed all of the requirements for your baccalaureate degree. I am pleased, therefore, to tell you that your name has been placed among those who will be certified to receive their degrees in January, 1977.

The diplomas for those who complete their degree requirements for January will be sent to our graduates by mail in May. The Recorder of the College has requested the Registrar to send your diploma to the above address. If you wish your diploma sent elsewhere, you may communicate a different address to the Assistant Registrar, Student Services Building, Room 108.

Congratulations on having completed the requirements for your baccalaureate degree, and best wishes for the future.

> *Sincerely,*

> *Dean, College of Arts and Sciences*

My uncle, Mugs Halas, saw the letter and was amused. He thought he would rattle my cage a little so he drafted a letter in response. I have translated my uncle's letter into polite language.

Dear Dean,

How the fudge can you write such a letter. If McCaskey has completed "all of the requirements" shucks, why can't the diploma be mailed right now?

Patrick McCaskey

His father and I spent countless hours trying to get Pat off his butt to complete the work. Now you bozos pull this. He was never a goof-off until he went to college.

We don't want the diploma.

Mugs Halas

Mugs's letter was never sent and I received the diploma. I enjoyed my time at Indiana and I have visited the school often.

Singing in Church
I like
to sing
in Church
because the people there
are more likely
to forgive me.
When I sing
in Church,
I pray
that God will help me sing better
so that
there will be less suffering
in the world.
    —Patrick McCaskey

Chapter 8: Martyrs Shrine

In the 1640s, French Jesuit missionaries, Father Isaac Jogues, René Goupil, and John Lalande were tortured and killed by the Mohawks in an Indian village called Ossernenon. These three, along with five Jesuit priests martyred in Canada, were canonized in 1930 as the North American Martyrs. The Mohawk village where the three deaths occurred was destroyed in time. To honor the martyrs, the church has built the Shrine of Our Lady of Martyrs in Auriesville, New York, which is said to be the birthplace of Blessed Kateri Tekakwitha and thought to be where the village stood.[38] The shrine is on the south bank of the Mohawk River.

---

38 Some suggest the actual village was miles away, but the purpose of the shrine is to have a prayerful place that celebrates the sacrifices of these martyrs from North American. Another Martyrs Shrine exists in Midland, Ontario, Canada, that celebrates the martyrs' lives for Canadians.

PILGRIMAGE

French Jesuits came to Canada in 1625 led by Father John de Brebeuf, who would become one of the North American Martyrs. They traveled to regions of Lake Huron to evangelize. Father Isaac Jogues joined Father Brebeuf in 1636. In July 1642, Father Jogues left for Quebec where he met René Goupil and accompanied by another missionary named William Couture, they set out on the Saint Lawrence River in canoes with 40 Algonquin and Huron Indians and a 13-year-old Catholic Huron named Theresa who was returning home after studying with the Ursuline sisters. They were ambushed by the Iroquois. Father Jogues, Rene Goupil, and William Couture were beaten, bound and taken captive. They traveled to the Mohawk Valley and the missionary captives were brutalized at individual settlements. They arrived at Ossernenon on August 14, 1642, the eve of the Feast of the Assumption of the Blessed Mother. They were beaten with clubs as they ran the gauntlet up a steep hill between two single files of braves then taken to a stage or platform to be burned, cut, and mutilated. Several of Father Jogues's fingers were either severed or maimed including his "canonical fingers" with which he held the Host during Mass.

Brutalities were inflicted at other villages, but Father Jogues, Goupil, and Couture survived as slaves. Father Jogues and Goupil were taken to Ossernenon, and Couture and Theresa to the other villages. Many native captives were absorbed into the tribe. This was the fate of Theresa. The Dutch superintendent of the area came to Ossernenon to negotiate the release of the three Frenchmen. Offers of ransom were unsuccessful.

One day, Goupil was struck on the head and killed by an Indian with a tomahawk. Father Jogues continued as a slave. Eventually, he escaped and was kept hidden until a ransom was accepted. He returned to France on

Christmas Day, 1643. Pope Urban VIII (1623-1644), learning of Father Jogues's request to celebrate Mass without the canonical fingers, gave him this special dispensation.

Father Jogues became a celebrity, but the attention given to him was not welcomed. After four months, he returned to Canada for a couple of years. Then, like Saint Patrick, he returned to his previous captors regardless of his fears. He journeyed to Ossernenon as a peace ambassador. Peace talks went well and he returned to Canada. On a second peace mission to Ossernenon, a few days walk from Ossernenon, his party was ambushed on the trail, bound, beaten, and taken captive. As he entered the longhouse of one of the clans, an Indian attacked him with a tomahawk taking his life. A missionary companion, John Lelande, was also killed. Both martyrs were beheaded, their heads placed on the palisades facing Canada as a warning to other Frenchmen, and their bodies were thrown into the Mohawk River. The Catholic faith took root in the New World because of the sacrifice of holy men and women.

Another person who sacrificed for the faith at the time in the New World was Kateri Tekakwitha, known as the Lily of the Mohawks. Born in 1656, Tekakwitha suffered from small pox and was badly scarred and nearly blinded by the disease. When the Jesuit missionaries returned to the Mohawk Valley to continue the work of Father Jogues, Tekakwitha was baptized. Persecuted for her convictions, she eventually fled to the Christian community of Caughnawaga in Montreal. She died at age 24. The facial scarring from the small pox disappeared upon her death, and people almost immediately began having visions of her and prayers answered through her intercession. Kateri Tekakwitha was beatified in 1980 and canonized a Saint on October 22, 2012 by Pope Benedict XVI (2005-2013).

Saint Isaac Jogues

Daily Mass

Don Nevins and I often volunteered to serve 6:30 a.m. daily Mass. One morning I complained to Sister Amata about having to get up so early. She calmly explained that she got up much earlier than I did.

Later in the day, she gave me a book entitled *Mangled Hands*. It was about Father Isaac Jogues. He was a missionary to the Iroquois Indians. They hacked off his thumbs with tomahawks. Yet he continued to try to convert them to Christianity. I didn't complain anymore. I went to daily Mass and I had a wonderful childhood.

After I had read about fifteen Scott Hahn books, I became convinced that it was a good idea to attend Mass as often as possible. So I've been going to daily Mass since July. I go to daily Mass and I am having a wonderful adulthood.

Resolution

State of Illinois

County of Lake

Whereas, Scott & Kimberly Hahn married each other on August 18, 1979, and

Whereas, Scott & Kimberly Hahn thrilled the nation with their invitation, and

Whereas, Scott & Kimberly Hahn are grateful for their six faithfully Catholic children and now fourteen grandchildren, and

Whereas, Scott & Kimberly Hahn have co-written the books Rome Sweet Rome and Life-Giving Love, and

Whereas, Scott & Kimberly Hahn have recorded audio cassettes "Catholic Marriage Covenant," "Life-Giving Love," "Secrets for Successful Evangelization," "Our Way to Rome," "The Venerable Beads," and "A Kingdom Divided," and

Whereas, Scott & Kimberly Hahn co-run their Catholic apostolate, the Saint Paul Center for Biblical Theology, and

Whereas, Scott & Kimberly Hahn do not regret any possible lost youth because those years were spent as Protestants.

Now therefore be it resolved that Sports Faith International does adopt this Resolution to honor and hold in high esteem Scott & Kimberly Hahn.

Adopted the eighteenth day of August, 2016.

—Patrick McCaskey

Thinking About Singing

When my father's father, Dick McCaskey, sang,
people cried
because his singing was so beautiful.
When I sing,
people cry for a different reason.
My mother's father, George Halas, sang
in the office
after five o'clock.
"From the East
and
from the West
they sent their very best
to play against the pride
of Old Chicago..."
My father, Ed McCaskey, used to sing
In the office
from nine to five.
Phil Foster said that
my father was the world's greatest unknown singer.
After I sing,
people say to me,
"We really miss your father."
When my sons' ages were in single digits,
We had bedtime concerts.
Some of the favorite songs were
"Bear Down, Chicago Bears," "If I Had A Hammer,"
"Five Hundred Miles," and "The Star Spangled Banner."
One night, my son, Ed, was so tired,
He said,
"The concert's over."
Sometimes I have to say to my sons,
"If you don't behave, I'll sing."
They reply,
"Okay Dad; we'll behave."
—Patrick McCaskey

Pilgrims on the Pennsylvania Turnpike

Thousands of young people coming home from the 2016 March for Life in Washington, DC, were stranded along with other travelers in a blizzard on the Pennsylvania Turnpike. Traffic stood still for about 24 hours. Busses of students from several Midwest states left the comfort of their vehicles and went around doing what they could for other stranded travelers—clearing snow off cars, sharing food, and inviting people to their buses to warm up. As the storm continued, a hearty contingent from Minnesota built an altar out of snow. The wind howled and the snow continued to fall as they finished their work.

Bill Dill from the Archdiocese of Saint Paul and Minneapolis knocked on Father Patrick Behm's bus door and told him that they had built an altar and asked if he would want to say mass. Father Behm of Le Mars, Iowa, later remarked, "Those Minnesotans really know how to build stuff out of snow!"

Father Behm acted as celebrant; it was he who had a travel Mass Kit! Father Behm and his students were on their way home to All Saints Parish and the Gehlen Catholic Schools in Le Mars.[39] Seven other priests concelebrated the Mass and they did their best to break up the Communion small enough to handle hundreds of communicants. By the time it came to pass out Communion, Father Behm's hands were numb and others stepped in to distribute the hosts.

---

[39] Joanne Fox, "Priest Celebrates Mass on Pennsylvania Turnpike," *The Catholic Globe*, January 29, 2016. Viewed at http://www.catholicglobe.org/?p=5712 on February 2, 2016.

When Father Behm got home, the Mass on the Pennsylvania Turnpike took on a media life of its own and the parish priest found himself in demand for interviews. In response to all the publicity, Father Behm said: "I'm just happy being a simple priest." Speaking about the March for Life and the storm, Father Behm said: "Christ was with us in this storm. He's with us in every storm, and it is He who will ultimately bring the victory."

Small School with Big Values

Catholic Central High School in Burlington, Wisconsin, began life as Saint Mary's High School about 95 years ago. Saint Mary's pastor, Father Van Treeck, and Sister Michael of the School Sisters of Notre Dame got things started. The school draws from several parishes in Burlington, Fontana, Delavan, East Troy, Elkhorn, Lake Geneva, New Munster, Union Grove, and Waterford. Despite its small size, Catholic Central offers a college prep program with ambitious sports offerings and many extracurricular activities. But perhaps the greatest benefit for students, is its life-long Catholic values and respect for other faiths that are instilled in its student body.

In football, Catholic Central competes in the smallest division in the State of Wisconsin and routinely vies well into the tournament brackets. In the last 8 years, Catholic Central played in the quarter finals twice (2011 and 2015), took a second place finish (2010), and won the championship (2009 and 2008). In 2008, the Hilltoppers had a perfect 14-0 season.

Routinely, about half the boys in the school play varsity football. A large percentage of football players include first and second honors recipients.

The school and its athletes are committed to serve in the community with faith-based education aid to younger children, highway cleanup, Burlington Historical Society work, and many other activities.

It is encouraging to know that the Catholic Central Football Team attends Sunday Mass together. Prayers are said before and after each contest. The Catholic Central Football Team was inducted into the Sports Faith International Hall of Fame.

A good program needs good leaders. Tom Aldrich, the Athletic Director and Head Football Coach at Catholic Central, was honored with the Sports Faith International "Hometown Hero" Award. Aldrich was also voted the All-Racine County Coach of the Year for the eighth time in 2015.

Fellow coaches pointed out that Aldrich develops players who are unselfish and he handles his players exceptionally. I had the honor of speaking at Catholic Central High School in Burlington, Wisconsin.

Focus on Football

Football is a wonderful game.
There's blocking and tackling
And much, much more.
As coaches,
We expect the players
To stay focused
For the whole season.
Then we hope
That they stay focused
For the rest
Of their lives.
If they are called
To the sacrament
Of Holy Orders,
We trust that they will be ordained,
During the offseason.
If they are called
To the sacrament
Of Matrimony,
We trust that they will get married,
During the offseason.
If they are blessed
With children,
We trust that they will be born,
During the offseason.
　　　　　—Patrick McCaskey

Saint Thomas Aquinas High School

The Saint Thomas Raiders Football Team in Fort Lauderdale carries its weight by completing as individuals a generous number of service hours. Fifteen local groups or agencies are the richer for having received the gift of time and talent shared by the team. Local churches and elementary schools, Pee Wee football, the Plantation Little League, and Women in Distress are among local groups helped.

The team is centered spiritually. Rooted in the Catholic tradition for 32 years, the squad prays outside the school chapel prior to every game. They pray as a team at pre game meals and after every game.

Routinely ranked as one of the top teams in the nation, Saint Thomas Aquinas has won the State Championship nine times as we go to press! In 2015, there were 17 former Saint Thomas students playing for the NFL—tops in the nation.[40] Former Chicago Bears running back Brian Piccolo, after whom Saint Thomas' football stadium is named, was the first Raider to play in the NFL. Piccolo died of cancer in 1970 and his story was told in the movie (two versions, 1971 and 2001) "Brian's Song." Piccolo's life certainly gives players added inspiration to become men who lead exemplary lives. The team shines in academics and includes National Merit Semifinalists, members of the National Honor Society, and members of the National Society of High School Scholars.

The light of Christ shines in the lives of the players, in every action they take. They go to Christ for guidance, reassurance, and comfort. He responds by helping them reach their full potential as human beings, Catholics, and athletes. All things are done through Christ, who makes all things possible. The team was named to the All Star Catholic High School Sports Faith Hall of Fame.

Amy McMahon's Love and Joy

Amy McMahon really loves the game of soccer. She brings that love and joy to the varsity soccer team at

---

[40] Dave Brousseau, "Saint Thomas Aquinas leads nation with 17 NFL players," *Sun Sentinel,* September 28, 2015, viewed at http://www.sun sentinel.com/sports/highschool/football/broward/fl-brow-football-notes-0924-20150923-story.html on August 12, 2016.

The Willows Academy in Des Plaines where she coaches. She is most proud of her team members who are all active members of the Respect Life Club at The Willows Academy and for their participation at March for Life in Washington, DC.

Amy attributes her success on the field to her Catholic Faith, which guides her as a coach, as a teacher and as an adult in general. McMahon says faith is a big part of sports at her school and that her team prays to a litany of saints before every game. She said that when they play another Catholic school they pray to the patron of the opposing team.

McMahon was inducted into the Sports Faith International All Star Catholic High School Hall of Fame.

Servite High School

The Servite High School Football Team won back-to-back Pac 5 Championships; they did it the right way, while staying true to their founders' principles and their Catholic faith. It is an all-boys Catholic school in Anaheim in Southern California that consistently wins through a very tough schedule. Servite's team has a champions' manual. Four formation themes are: Primacy of faith, Mastery of self, Necessity of others, and Centrality of Christ. Winning focuses on love for your fellow man and doing the right things.

The school curriculum tests the college-bound student. Servite students are challenged to be Christ to others and see Christ in others. Each student must complete 100 hours of Christian Community Service over their 4 years.

The 2010 Servite Football Team ranked 7th in the nation. They were 14–1 with their only loss being to the

#1 team in the nation De La Salle in the State Championship game.[41] They won their league championship for the 6th straight year and won their section championship for the 2nd year in a row.

Servite High School forms faith filled leaders; Coaches work to see their players become the men that God has called them to be.

The coaches say that they learn so much more from the young men each and every year than what they are teaching them. They are a great group of men. They are the men from Servite.

---

[41] De La Salle is a perennial national powerhouse and its 2010 Coach Bob Ladouceur's career was examined in Patrick McCaskey's, *Sports and Faith: More Stories of the Devoted and the Devout* (Crystal Lake, IL, Sporting Chance Press, 2015) 107-108.

Chapter 9: Canterbury

One of England's greatest men, Saint Thomas Becket, was born in London in 1118. Becket was well educated and worked as a clerk and accountant. Later, he studied law. Becket quarreled with King Henry II and he was murdered in the Canterbury Cathedral on December 29, 1170.

Thomas Becket joined the household of Theobold, the Archbishop of Canterbury, who became his patron. Becket became Archdeacon of Canterbury and then King Henry II made him chancellor. Becket was a close friend and companion of the King. Becket also enjoyed a lavish lifestyle. Thoroughly in the King's corner, Becket enjoyed his positions and the rights and privileges that came with them.

At the time, a movement called Gregorian Reform was gaining momentum. Gregorian Reform fostered the moral integrity and independence of the clergy. It promoted free elections to clerical posts, the sacredness of church property, freedom of appeal to Rome, and clerical immunity from civil courts. The Church wanted to control its clergy and move away from civil authorities' control.

When Theobold died, Henry II wanted Becket to become the Archbishop of Canterbury. Becket encouraged Henry to select someone else. He was concerned and many scholars suggest that he saw his duties change as Archbishop. But Henry saw that Becket became the new Archbishop. Becket seemed predisposed to his king's views, but with his new responsibilities he suddenly made an about-face and took the side of the Church and Rome. Moving away from worldliness, he became devout.

The situation was complicated. Henry II was falling back on how things had been formerly arranged in England under Henry I. Henry II issued the Constitutions of Clarendon, documents that drew a line in the sand and asserted the King's right to punish criminal clerks, forbid excommunication of royal officials and appeals to Rome, and give the King the revenues of vacant sees and the power to influence episcopal elections. At first, Becket agreed to the Constitutions of Clarendon, but then he revoked his agreement. Thereafter, Henry and Becket were in opposition.

When Henry went to prosecute Becket, the Archbishop left for France. When Becket returned years later after a truce had been made, more conflict between his office and Henry's returned. Henry voiced his frustrations: "Will no one rid me of this troublesome priest!" Four knights, "perhaps" taking Henry's wish literally, famously slew the Archbishop in the Canterbury Cathedral.

PILGRIMAGE

Within a couple years after the death of Thomas Becket, Pope Alexander III (1159-1181) canonized him. Becket's burial place at Canterbury became a popular place of pilgrimage. Henry II was an early pilgrim. Relics of Becket were collected and people who came into contact with them were cured of disease. The faithful making the pilgrimage to Canterbury were given a medal badge with the symbol of the Becket Shrine. Monks placed Becket's marble coffin in the crypt of the Cathedral and built a wall with gaps in it that permitted pilgrims to kiss the Saint's final resting place. The wall protected the coffin from theft.

In 1220, Becket's bones were moved behind the high altar and placed on a raised platform supported by pillars. Canterbury was already a place visited by pilgrims, but after Becket's death pilgrimages grew rapidly.

In the last century, Becket's story was dramatized by T.S. Elliot in his play, *Murder in the Cathedral*. Elliot uses a chorus like classic Greek plays and he explores the Saint's internal conflicts as his death approaches. Elliot's play was written as fascism was growing before World War II. Elliot taps into the rich tapestry of the Becket story and looks at four temptations similar to those of Christ. The fourth tempter tells Becket to seek martyrdom for the glory of it. A temptation that is described as "the greatest treason: To do the right deed for the wrong reason."

At the time of the Reformation, Henry VIII, who broke away from the Catholic Church in England, had Becket's bones and his shrine destroyed. Henry VIII was an advocate for royal rights over the church and had battled his own Becket-like figure, Thomas More, the Lord Chancellor. More opposed Henry's annulment of marriage to Catherine of Aragon and believed the

Reformation to be heretical. Like Becket, More was killed for his views. Thomas More was canonized a saint in 1935.

Chaucer's Canterbury Tales

Geoffrey Chaucer wrote a collection of stories in Middle English called *The Canterbury Tales* during a tumultuous period of English history. But rather than reflect the gloom that people may have felt at the time, Chaucer chose to have some fun with a variety of weighty subjects. For his setting, he chose a pilgrimage journey from London to the Canterbury Cathedral, home of the Shrine of Saint Thomas Becket. Today's readers will find something of Mel Brooks and Monty Python in Chaucer's stories.

Storytelling was popular during Chaucer's time. Pilgrims on the journey compete in a story-telling contest; such contests were also popular. The stories highlight the human weaknesses and the corruption of the times. The work reveals Chaucer's humorous thoughts on a variety of social issues. It is a masterpiece in English Literature.

During Chaucer's early life, the Black Death had scourged Europe and it had an effect on the way people looked at faith.[42] Competing Popes, false relics, the sale of indulgences, and many other types of corruption appeared in various classes of people including the Religious.[43] And it did not matter how sacred a position a character in the tales held, Chaucer was often taking

---

[42] Black Death was a devastating pandemic that claimed many millions of Europeans and it took hundreds of years for the population to recover.

[43] Relics were of great value, both spiritually and monetarily in the Middle Ages. In fact, historians look at fraud and theft of relics as inevitable at the time. See Morris Bishop, The Middle Ages (American Heritage Library) (Boston: Houghton Mifflin, 1968, 1987) 146-149.

them down several pegs. Chaucer worked in various "government" offices and he was a courtier. He was a friend, an employee, and a relative to royalty. *The Canterbury Tales* was one of several works written by the author. His writings were produced in manuscript form because the printing press was not invented until the middle of the 15th century, roughly 50 years after the writer's death.

Chaucer's *The Canterbury Tales* had people of different social classes come together on the pilgrimage. The Inn Keeper of the guesthouse where the tales begin serves as the host and the judge of the contest. The Knight maintains the honored traditions in his story. The Miller is a drunken vulgar man who tells a mocking tale of a carpenter. The Reeve, a manager of a large estate, who was a carpenter, plays off the Miller's Tale in rough fashion. The Man of Law tells a romantic story of a Christian princess and a Sultan. There is a Cook who provides a partial story of perversion.

The Wife of Bath, a woman with five husbands, tells a story that examines the desires of women. A Friar, who loves taverns and food, tells a story critical of a Summoner, one who calls people to church trials and is often corrupt. The Summoner gets back at the Friar with his story. The Clerk's story is one of faithfulness in opposition to the Wife of Bath's. The Merchant shares a tale of marriage. A Squire, a lady's man has a fragmented tale of love. A Franklin, a wealthy land owner who knows the good life, tells of a noble woman and a dilemma. A Shipman tells a tale of money, business, and sex. A Prioress tells a tale of a young Christian murdered by Jews, mirroring an entire class of anti-Semitic stories of the day. The Monk's Tale is a series of tragedies that gets tiring. The Physician's Tale is a tragic story of a father and his daughter.

A Pardoner is present and he is a person who sells indulgences and relics. He tells a tale of three men who fight over newfound wealth. The Pardoner cheats people out of their money, but at the same time he encourages others to repent for their sins, although he is unapologetic for his own failings. The Nun's Priest tells an uplifting story of a rooster who is seized by a fox who plays on the rooster's vanity. When the rooster escapes, the fox tries again to play on his vanity, but the rooster has learned his lesson. The Second Nun, a much more pious one than the first, tells the story of Saint Cecilia, a saint who encourages her pagan husband to become Christian. The Manciple, in this case a purchasing agent for a law school, tells a story about a man's crow who discloses his wife's infidelity and the tragedy that unfolds. The Parson is a good member of the clergy and his tale is a sermon.

Chaucer's Tales are open to interpretation and that is one aspect of them that has been popular. Despite the faults and failings of the pilgrims, the fact that all are on a pilgrimage suggests an effort for redemption. Chaucer ends his tales by expressing remorse for his various works that have offended God and asks his readers to pray that Christ has mercy on him and forgives his sins.

Chaucer

Chaucer, "pitee renneth soone in gentil herte"
Many scholars have devoted their lives
To the study of Chaucer.
Their studious research has enabled me
To write this frivolous poem.
Chaucer was an ambassador
From England
To Italy and France.
He knew their languages and their literatures.
He had the courage to write humor
After the Black Death (1348-1349) and
During the Hundred Years War (1346-1446).
He wrote as an avocation and
Gave readings
At Court.
His writings were not published
In his lifetime (1340?-1400)
Because the printing press had not been
invented (1440).
Chaucer became more religious
In his later life,
But perhaps as a youth
He was an altar boy
Who goofed around a little
During Mass.
More research is needed
In this area.
                              —Patrick McCaskey

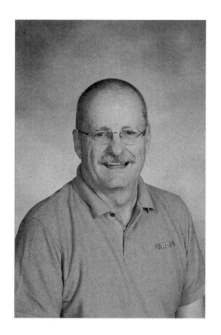

A Man for All Seasons at Carmel

Carmel Catholic High School is a college preparatory and secondary school for young men and women. It is located in Lake County, Illinois, amidst an abundance of Catholic institutions such as the University of Saint Mary of the Lake Seminary; Marytown, the National Shrine of Saint Maximilian Kolbe; WSFI Catholic Radio; monasteries; retreat houses; and other such institutions.

Carmel provides a quality Catholic education and is committed to meeting the academic, physical, social and spiritual needs of the students it serves. Mike Fitzgibbons is tuned into the students at Carmel. And you have to love Mike Fitzgibbons. He is one of those guys who loves his job working with high school kids and he has been doing it for over 40 years. Mike has taught English and Religion at Carmel. He has coached football, wrestling, and track. And he has been a Campus Minister at the School. He is also a Licensed Clinical Professional Counselor. But for Fitzgibbons, each day has been a blessing, something that he has enjoyed. And it shows.

Fitzgibbons has also published a novel called *My Senior Year* and he has a book of poems called *The Light Within*. Mike also created a film called "From Yesterday Till Tomorrow." Fitzgibbons is a speaker and runs team-building workshops. He and his wife have raised three children, Molly, Michael, and Kevin.

But for all Fitzgibbons's accomplishments, when he stood up to accept his induction into the Sports Faith International Hall of Fame he looked out at the audience and said, "I don't know why I am here." And then he went on to explain himself by saying he has been lucky, in that every day he loved his work and was happy to be doing it. In other words, for Fitzgibbons it was more a pleasure than a struggle and he felt a little humbled to be honored with professional athletes and others at the event.

Of course, many people realize that to be a teacher is not an easy task. To be a decent coach is not a piece of cake. And to help others through counseling can be very difficult. To do it all for many years as Fitzgibbons has done with grace and good spirits is remarkable.

Letter from Other Women

March 3, 2014

Gretchen Wagle McCaskey

Dear Gretchen,

This is Sheila. I met Pat in 1958. We were in third grade together at Saint Mary's in Des Plaines. When he was passing out the milk cartons, I asked him for an extra carton.

When we were in eighth grade, he kept asking me to dance. I tried to teach him how to cha cha cha, but he doesn't have the gift of dancing. I had to tell him that he should dance with other girls.

I went to Maine West High School. Pat called me after his football games to let me know what he did. During one of his pauses, I was able to interject, "I was elected homecoming queen."

I married Charlie in 1973. Pat was there. We danced together at the reception, but he still wasn't a very good dancer.

This is Mary Jo. I met Pat in 1962. He was taking swimming and diving lessons at Rand Park in Des Plaines. He wasn't a very good swimmer or a very good diver.

I was a cheerleader for Saint Stephen's in Des Plaines. We beat Saint Mary's 26-23 at Notre Dame High School. We also beat them twice at Rand Park.

PILGRIMAGE

This is Louise. I went to Mary Seat of Wisdom in Park Ridge. We beat Saint Mary's 46-37 at Notre Dame High School in the playoffs. Pat fouled out of the game.

I met Pat the summer after eighth grade in 1963. Sheila introduced me to him.

I started out at Marywood High School in Evanston. After my family moved to Wheaton, I went to Saint Francis High School.

When we were high school juniors, he rode his bike 25 miles from Des Plaines to Wheaton to see me. I wasn't home.

This is Karen. I went to Regina High School. I met Pat at a Notre Dame High School sock hop. He said to me, "After I get my driver's license, I'm going to ask you for a date."

Pat wasn't a very good dancer. He did take me to the movies.

This is Maureen. I met Pat when we were high school sophomores in 1964. I was a cheerleader for Immaculate Conception High School in Elmhurst.

He took the train from Des Plaines to Chicago to Elmhurst to see me. Then he reversed the process.

After he got his driver's license, he drove me to his prom. He didn't take me to the picnic the day after the prom because he had a track meet. He called me to let me know the results of the meet, but I wasn't interested.

This is Peggy. I went to Marywood High School. I met Pat when we were high school sophomores in 1964. Louise introduced me to him. He said to me, "After I get my driver's license, I'm going to ask you for a date."

Two years later, he drove me to the Bismarck Theatre in Chicago to see the movie "Doctor Zhivago." He drove the wrong way down a one way street. I hope that you are helping him with his driving. I went with him to his sister Ellen's wedding. We didn't go to the reception because he had a track meet.

I married Danny in 1974. Pat was the lector at our wedding. I asked him to sing at our wedding, but he felt that he wasn't a good enough singer.

This is Marcy. I went to Chippewa Junior High School in Des Plaines. Then I went to Maine West High School. I sat in front of Pat when he came to Chippewa basketball games. I kept turning around to talk to him, but he kept telling me to watch the game.

Pat and I dated in the summer of 1967 and the summer of 1968. Is he still upset because he couldn't play college football?

This is Mary. My grandmother and Pat's grandmother were best friends. They lived around the corner from each other in Lancaster, Pennsylvania.

My parents have eleven children: eight girls and three boys. You probably know that Pat's parents have eleven children: eight boys and three girls.

I met Pat at my parents' home. He gave piggy back rides to my brothers and sisters. My mother liked him, but I didn't.

This is Liz. I met Pat in 1968. I was traveling from Vassar to my roommate's home over break. Pat was traveling from Cheshire Academy to Paoli, Pennsylvania to visit his uncle Jim and his family.

Pat and I dated in the summer of 1968 and the summer of 1970. I lived in Homewood. Pat tried to drive to my house without using the toll way so he wouldn't have to pay tolls. He got lost and he was very late.

My sister, Cortney, said to him, "I'll give you a quarter for the toll."

Pat replied, "It's four tolls each way."

Cortney said, "Forget it."

This is Anita. Pat and my brother, Ted, were summer baseball teammates in Des Plaines. Pat wasn't very good in baseball, but my brother was. I went to Maine West High School and Northwestern University.

Pat and I dated in the winter and spring of 1969. When I visited him at Indiana University, we went caving with the guys on his McNutt Quad dorm floor. I got very muddy. That might have been our last date.

Like Pat, all of us were born in 1949 and we graduated from high school in 1967. We think it was a good idea for Pat to marry a younger woman because he was immature. All of us are grateful to you for taking him off our hands. Thank you for marrying him. Best wishes on your 30th anniversary

      The Grateful Ten

Sheila, Mary Jo, Louise, Peggy, Maureen, Karen, Mary, Marcy, Liz, Anita

Sean McGovern: Virtue

Dan Duddy is the football coach at Monsignor Donovan High School in Toms River, New Jersey.[44] Duddy's entire football team and coaching staff go away to "Virtue Camp" every year before the season starts. At

---

[44] His exceptional story was told in Sports and Faith: More Stories of the Devoted and the Devout (2015).

camp, and throughout the season, virtues are examined and encouraged including discipline, concentration, respect for school rules, excellence in effort of competition, leadership, confidence, fair play, teamwork, sacrifice, determination, resilience, and respect for others.

When you play for Dan Duddy, you have plenty of great examples around you including the coaches as well as fellow players. This is not lost on Coach Duddy. Duddy nominated one of his players, Sean McGovern, for the Sports Faith Virtue of Saint Paul Award that he received in 2012. Dan wrote, "Sean is a product of our Virtue Program through football. He is one of seven siblings in a family with no father. He is the oldest son and the leader. He was an outstanding leader for his football team and is a very spiritual and virtuous Catholic young man. Sean is among the very best young men in virtue that I have coached in 32 years."

Duddy works hard to teach virtues like sacrifice, determination, and resilience to his players. When you have a Sean McGovern on the team, it's all too evident how important these can be in life. One day a virtue might mean a win or loss on the field. Later, it contributes to a life well lived for the right reasons.

From Toms River, McGovern moved on to Syracuse University to earn a degree in Information Management and Technology. McGovern is a member of Sigma Phi Epsilon Fraternity, which was created on biblical principles and has a mission to "Building Balanced Men," which is achieved through a commitment to a sound mind and a sound body. McGovern retains his love of sports and spends time these days on personal fitness rather than competitive play. He maintains his faith and fondly remembers his coaches, teachers, and students at Monsignor Donovan. McGovern's mother recently remarried and his family now lives in Buffalo. McGovern goes back to Toms River to visit Coach Duddy and he takes his virtues with him everywhere he goes.

Abraham Was Not on the Tonight Show

Here's a poem that I wrote before I got married:

Sharing

> If you have something worthwhile
> To share,
> People will hear
> Of it.
> Abraham and Moses and Jesus were never even
> On The Tonight Show
> For heaven's sake (a good cause).
> My shares are less than theirs.
> So I'm delighted to be here.
> I don't want to begin my public life
> Until I'm thirty.
> That was the age of Jesus
> When He started.
> I'll save my money
> In case
> Of marriage
> Or some other act
> Of God.
> I'd like to get married
> When I'm thirty-three.
> That was the age of Jesus
> When the Romans crucified Him.
> That was also the age of Christ
> When He rose from the dead.
> Marriage is a middle-ground
> Not the Promised Land.
> —Patrick McCaskey

My Funeral Arrangements

When I die, I hope that everyone will be wracked with grief and unable to work on my funeral arrangements. So I've written this essay to help you. I feel fine and I hope that this is long range planning.

When I was a student at Saint Mary's School in Des Plaines, Illinois, the nuns used to sit the students who misbehaved next to the students who behaved. The students who behaved would be a good influence on the students who misbehaved.

Don Nevins often sat next to me. Now he is an excellent priest. When I got married, he was the priest. When my children were baptized, he was the priest. He has agreed to say my funeral.

After Father Ryan said the funeral of Diane Shabat's father, I said to him, "You did very well Father, but Father Nevins has already agreed to say my funeral."

Father Ryan asked, "Can I be a concelebrant?"

I replied, "Yes."

He said, "I'll gather your grandchildren around your casket."

Father Peter Armenio has also asked to be a concelebrant. That would be fine. He's from New Jersey like my wife, Gretchen. He also played football.

John Haben of Haben Funeral Home has agreed to coordinate my wake and funeral at Saint Mary's Church in Lake Forest. Please don't have any fights in the parking lot.

Barb Love McCaskey has agreed to sing at my funeral. She will sing "Softly & Tenderly," "Blessed Are," and "Finally Home." If Barb predeceases me, I guess I'll have to get someone else.

For the Old Testament reading, I would like the Commandments. For the New Testament reading, I would like the Beatitudes. I'd like two of my sons to be lectors.

Gretchen and I have been blessed with three fine sons: Ed, Tom, and Jim. We've also been blessed with at least three fine nephews. I'd like my sons and my nephews to be my pallbearers. To represent Gretchen's side of the family, Chad, Matt, and Brandon Bradley would be very good pallbearers. I'd like my pallbearers to wear patrol belts. I have written my remembrance. After Communion, I'd like one of my sons to read it.

Mark Twain

Chapter 10: Literary Pilgrimages

I have a number of favored authors who have provided me and millions of others with great thoughts and entertainment. I have traveled on "Literary" Pilgrimages to see the historic places of these authors and I enjoyed getting a firsthand look.

Earl Hamner Junior

Earl Hamner Junior was born on July 10, 1923 in Schuyler, Virginia. He went to the University of Richmond, Northwestern University, and the University of Cincinnati. He married Jane Martin on October 16, 1954.

Hamner's parents were hard-working people who inspired him to seek an education. His family served as the models for some of his most beloved characters. Hamner began writing for radio shortly after World War II. He started to develop novels and wrote for television as it was becoming popular. In the 1960s, Rod Serling used Hamner's work for "The Twilight Zone." According to Hamner:

I was raised on folk songs and folk stories, and I suppose it was inevitable that this kind of material worked its way into my writing. Several times I was able to use folk material in my Twilight Zone episodes, and I thought it courageous of Rod to accept this 'offbeat' kind of storytelling. Looking back, I realize that if I made any unique contribution to the series, it was to introduce the American folklore element into it.[45]

Hamner wrote the novel *Spenser's Mountain* which led to the movie of the same name. He also wrote the novel *The Homecoming* which led to the television series "The Waltons." Hamner was a modern author in that he often wrote for books and television, and sometimes developed his own programs. His themes and characters were often based on solid values that reminded viewers and readers of times past. The Waltons had 50 million

---

[45] From Earl Hamner's website viewed at http://www.earlhamner.com/about.html on January 4, 2016.

viewers and portrayed a humble and loving rural family making its way through The Depression and beyond. Hamner also wrote the screenplays for "Heidi" and "Charlotte's Web." He wrote and developed "Falcon Crest" and "Apple's Way" and he wrote episodes for "Gentle Ben" and "Nanny and the Professor."

There are millions of Waltons fans from around the world. His biographer, James E. Person, author of *Earl Hamner: From Walton's Mountain to Tomorrow*, wrote "Earl held to his vision of television and motion pictures as media for affirming the better angels of our nature..."

In 2013, I made a literary pilgrimage to Hamner's hometown of Schuyler. It's about thirty miles south of Charlottesville. There is a museum and visitors can walk through his childhood home. Hamner died on March 24, 2016, after a long successful life.

Walton Ways in McCaskey Household

I was a big fan of Earl Hamner and especially liked the Waltons. I can remember a simpler time when my parents, my 10 siblings, and I had plenty of chores and responsibilities like the Waltons to take care of in our home in Des Plaines. And then there was Lancaster, Pennsylvania and the Amish...

Amish Life in Lancaster, Pennsylvania

More Fun Than A Barnraising

My father grew up
In Lancaster, Pennsylvania.
My brother Mike, my brother Tim,
And my sister Ellen were born there.
For Christmas, 1975,
My parents gave us a book
On the Amish in Lancaster County.
On October 2, 1990,
My father was the honoree
At the American Ireland Fund Dinner.
It was a gala, social event.
My wife, Gretchen, had felt pressured
To get a new dress.
I remembered the Amish book.
It has wonderful pictures
With pertinent Bible quotes.
Below a picture
Of an Amish lady
In a plain, sack dress
Was the quote,
"And be not conformed to this world;
But be ye transformed
By the renewing of your mind...."
My wife renewed her mind,
Found an escape clause
In the family budget,
And bought a new dress.
   —Patrick McCaskey

John Powers

John Powers was born on Mark Twain's birthday, November 30, 1945 in Chicago. He had diplomas from Brother Rice High School, Loyola University Chicago, and Northwestern University. I saw him the first time he was ever on a stage at a comedy club in Chicago. He performed material from his book *The Last Catholic in America* about the differences between Catholics and "Publics."

Powers described his well-loved novels as books on the "Catholic Way of Life." He said that he was not seeking to cast either a positive or negative view on that way of life. Powers books were fictionalized memoirs of his childhood on the South Side of Chicago. He created humorous time capsules of the 1950s and 1960s when he went to school. They were written and released during the tumultuous times of social change in the 1970s, a period when many people longed for the simpler times his books covered. His *The Last Catholic in America, Do Patent Leather Shoes Really Reflect Up,* and *The Unoriginal Sinner and the Ice Cream God* make up his trilogy of the times. Powers was able to capture those times in a human way that only made the era more meaningful to those who lived through it.

Powers was also a motivational speaker and writer. On Saturday, January 8, 1994, I heard John speak at a men's ecumenical breakfast in Lake Forest, Illinois. Among many other worthwhile things, he said, "Each of us in this room, every morning when we awake, we have before us this gift which we call life. Through our love of living, and the love of ourselves, the love of the people in our lives, we learn to unwrap that gift so that we can discover all the beauty and the challenge and the excitement that that gift holds for each of us. Only then can we give it to those around us. Because you cannot give what you have not got."

Powers lived with his family in Lake Geneva, Wisconsin. My wife, Gretchen, and our children and I were guests in their home. He died on January 17, 2013.

Gifts Galore

A true gift is really two gifts.
The first gift is the gift.
The second gift is no requirement
Of a thank-you note.
If you get thanked,
That's your second gift.
Your first gift is the gift
Of giving.
Your third gift is the end
Of this poem.
Every day is a gift.
—Patrick McCaskey

Carl Sandburg

Carl August Sandburg was born of Swedish immigrants on January 6, 1878. He quit school after completing eighth grade in 1891 and he went to work. Among other things, he delivered milk; harvested ice; laid bricks; and labored on farms before traveling as a hobo in 1897. After military service (without action) in the Spanish American War, he enrolled at Lombard College (now Knox College), joined a literary club, and supported himself with work as a fireman. At Lombard College, he played basketball. A few years later he married Lillian "Paula" Steichen in 1908.

PILGRIMAGE

Sandburg was an ambitious optimistic writer who looked forward to the future. Once he learned to play the guitar, he was also an entertainer. Garrison Keillor called him a "performing literary man."[46] He first published three books of poetry: *Reckless Ecstasy* (1904), *Incidentals* (1907), and *The Plaint of a Rose* (1908)—printed by his college professor, Phillip Green Wright.

Sandburg worked as a traveling salesman and then as a journalist for the *Chicago Daily News*, which helped provide him with rich experiences that he used for his writing. A group of his poems appeared in a popular poetry magazine and publication of his *Chicago Poems* (1916) brought him international praise.

He followed with *Cornhuskers* (1918) and *Smoke and Steel* (1920). He also wrote children's books: *Rootabaga Stories* (1922), *Rootabaga Pigeons* (1923), and *Potato Face* (1930). Sandburg wrote a two volume masterpiece entitled *Abraham Lincoln: The Prairie Years*, published in 1926. Sandburg's *The American Songbag* (folk music anthology, 1927) and another poetry book called *Good Morning America* (1928) followed. Four additional volumes published in 1940, *Abraham Lincoln: The War Years*, for which he won the Pulitzer Prize. Carl Sandburg was the Illinois Poet Laureate. Sandburg continued writing poems; *Remembrance Rock*, a novel; and some autobiographical materials. Sandburg's *Complete Poems* won him a second Pulitzer Prize in 1951.

The Sandburg home at 4646 North Hermitage Avenue in Chicago has a marker of distinction. The family lived at 331 South York Street in Elmhurst,

---

[46] Garrison Keillor, Introduction to *American Songbag*, Harcourt Brace and Company, 1990, page vii.

Illinois, in the fall of 1919. From his biography of Abraham Lincoln, we know that when Abraham Lincoln was mad at someone, he wrote that person a letter. Then he never mailed it.

The Sandburgs lived on a goat farm in Flat Rock, North Carolina, from 1945 through 1967. I have visited his Connemara Farm, which is now a National Park located on 264 acres. Visitors can tour the home, hike on over 5 miles of trails, and see the farm and descendants of Sandburg's dairy goats. Sandburg died at his home on July 22, 1967. He is buried at his birthplace in Galesburg.

Sandburg and Halas

On Tuesday, September 23, 1997, the city of Chicago designated 20 locations as markers of distinction. One of the places was where Carl Sandburg lived, 4646 North Hermitage Avenue. Another place was where my grandfather, George Halas, lived when he started the Bears, 4356 West Washington Boulevard. "Papa Bear" was synonymous with the Chicago Bears for a half-century as owner, coach, and general manager. He helped found the National Football League and turn pro football into mass entertainment.

When my grandfather was in the Navy during World War II, my grandmother Min, my uncle Mugs, and my mother lived at 5555 North Sheridan Road in Chicago. My grandfather lived there until he died in 1983. I visited there many times.

Sandburg and Halas were very good athletes. They also loved Chicago. Sandburg's poem about Chicago was published in 1914. It begins:

Hog butcher for the World,
Tool maker, Stacker of Wheat,

PILGRIMAGE

Player with Railroads and the Nation's Freight
Handler,
Stormy, husky brawling,
City of the Big Shoulders...

Here is an update:

Football team for the World,
Deal Maker, Stacker of Bucks,
Where expressways are always under
construction,
Aggressive, assertive,
City of the Shoulder Pads...

Sandburg's Rock Cut Farm

Scott Sanders

Scott Sanders was born on October 26, 1945. When he was 16, he met Ruth Ann McClure at a summer science camp. For 5 years, they wrote to each other. They saw each other maybe a dozen times. He went to Brown University on a physics scholarship. They married each other in 1967.

He earned a doctorate in literature at Cambridge University on another scholarship. He started teaching at Indiana University in 1971. He is a prolific writer—he has published 20 books and many essays and articles. He writes on nature and conservation, social justice, the relation between culture and geography, and the search for a spiritual path. His latest books include: *A Private History of Awe* (memoir), *A Conservationist Manifesto*, *Earth Works: Selected Essays*, and *Divine Animal* (a novel). I was in his writing class in the fall of 1973. He is a great teacher and a wonderful writer. He also gives readings from his writings.

My family and I have been guests in his home. He and his family have been guests in my home.

In his essay "Letter to a Reader," he wrote, "My steady desire has been to wake up, not to sleepwalk through this brief miraculous life. I wish to go about with mind and senses alert to the splendor of the world. I wish to see the burning bush."

Honor Him

Solomon wrote "The Song of Songs."
Professor Higgins sang "A Hymn to Him."
I can carry a tune,
But I need a bucket.
Samuel says the Lord declares,
"Those who honor me,
I shall honor."
What do you say?
I try and say different things.
Swear words are clichés.
Willie Mays was the say hey kid.
Thomas More was a man for all seasons.
Positive role models abound
In the Bible
And
On the street.
Eric Liddell lauded the Lord
And
God gave him a chariot of fire.
I fear the Lord
And close this poem,
Before I draw His ire.
—Patrick McCaskey

James Thurber

James Thurber was born on December 8, 1894 in Columbus, Ohio. He went to Ohio State University. He wrote and worked for the *New Yorker* magazine. He had severe eye problems and eventually went blind.

Thurber created 30 volumes of humor, fiction, children's books, cartoons, and essays. Thurber wrote and illustrated such popular books as *The Thurber*

Carnival and *My Life and Hard Times*, which have appeared in dozens of languages throughout the world. His short story, *The Secret Life of Walter Mitty*, has been read by students in anthologies for many decades and was made into two movies, one with Danny Kaye in 1947 and one with Ben Stiller in 2013.

My favorite Thurber fable is "The Little Girl and the Wolf." At the end, "the little girl took an automatic out of her basket and shot the wolf dead. Moral: It's not so easy to fool little girls nowadays as it used to be."

He performed a revue of his works on Broadway. He died on November 2, 1961. In the *New Yorker* obituary, E. B. White wrote:

It was fortunate that we got on well; the office we shared was the size of a hall bedroom. There was just room enough for two men, two typewriters, and a stack of copy paper. The copy paper disappeared at a scandalous rate—not because our production was high (although it was) but because Thurber used copy paper as the natural receptacle for discarded sorrows, immediate joys, stale dreams, golden prophecies, and messages of good cheer to the outside world and to fellow-workers. His mind was never at rest, and his pencil was connected to his mind by the best conductive tissue I have ever seen in action. The whole world knows what a funny man he was, but you had to sit next to him day after day to understand the extravagance of his clowning, the wildness and subtlety of his thinking, and the intensity of his interest in others and his sympathy for their dilemmas— dilemmas that he instantly enlarged, put in focus, and made immortal, just as he enlarged and made immortal, the strange goings on in the Ohio home of his boyhood.

PILGRIMAGE

His childhood home, 77 Jefferson Avenue, in Columbus, Ohio, is now a museum. Writers-in-residence and education programs are offered there.[47] In 2012, I visited there. It was quite a thrill to read Thurber books in the Thurber House.

Honor Him Again

Here is some Concordant advice.
Honor God
And
He will honor you.

Honor your father and your mother
And
You will have a long life
In the Lord.

Honor yourself
And
You will be humbled.
Humble yourself
And
You will be honored.

If you are a prophet,
Do not expect honor
In your own country
And
In your own home.

If you honor The Son,
You honor The Father
Who sent Him.
    —Patrick McCaskey

---

[47] See http://thurberhouse.org/ for details.

Mark Twain

Mark Twain was born Samuel Clemens on November 30, 1835 in Florida, Missouri. He grew up in Hannibal, Missouri, a port city on the banks of the Mississippi with boats heading south for Saint Louis and New Orleans. After his father died, Twain worked for his brother Orion's newspaper and left at age 17 to become a Riverboat Pilot. His pen name, Mark Twain, is a river term which means two fathoms or 12-feet deep, which was signaled to suggest that a boat is safe to go forward and not bottom out. During the Civil War, Twain became a newspaper reporter. He married Olivia Langdon and they had four children, but sadly only one survived past her 20s.

Twain was a major American author who would be known around the world. His stories were both humorous and sometimes they offered a commentary on social and political ills. His story, "The Celebrated Jumping Frog of Calaveras County" appeared in the *New York Saturday Press* on November 18, 1865 originally as "Jim Smiley and His Jumping Frog." His first book, *The Innocents Abroad*, was published in 1869. His classic tales, *The Adventures of Tom Sawyer* (1876) and *The Adventures of Huckleberry Finn* (1885) followed. He wrote 28 books and many short stories, letters and sketches.

Twain created his own publishing company and kept pouring money into a moveable typesetting machine. He went bankrupt and he felt honor-bound to repay his creditors. So he went on a world-wide lecture tour that he did not enjoy, but he was well-received. He paid his debts and he went a little goofy because of family tragedies.

I know Twain as a performer because of the Hal Holbrook performances and recordings. When I am forced into hearing a person talk incessantly, I remember a Twain line. "It's a terrible death to be talked to death."

He also said, "When we get to heaven, we will study and study and study, and progress and progress and progress, and if that isn't Hell, I don't know what is." Twain died on April 21, 1910 in Redding, Connecticut.

The Mark Twain House and Museum, a National Historic Landmark in Hartford, Connecticut, was the home of Twain and his family from 1874 to 1891. I have been there several times. He wrote most of his important works there. The striking 25-room home features a glass conservatory, a library, and a billiard room.

Missed Assignment

By Saturday at two,
I was prepared to lector at five.
But first a little nap.
No need to set the alarm.
If I miss this assignment,
The good priests will break my arm.
At 5:20 I awoke and knew
How Adam felt
After he had eaten the apple.
I erred
Which is human.
The good priests have forgiven
Which is divine.
                —Patrick McCaskey

E. B. White

E. B. White was born on July 11, 1899 in Mount Vernon, New York. He graduated from Cornell University. He wrote and worked for the *New Yorker* magazine. He had an aversion to public speaking. He never accepted his many awards in person. Two performances that White did give were the readings of two of his children's classics, *Charlotte's Web* and *The Trumpet of the Swan*. His third popular children's book is *Stuart Little*.

E.B. White authored 20 books of prose and poetry and he also wrote essays and drew sketches for the *New Yorker* magazine.[48] His books for adults include: *One Man's Meat, The Second Tree from the Corner, Letters of E. B. White, The Essays of E. B. White,* and *Poems and Sketches of E. B. White*.

When I was a student at Indiana University, I was an English major, but I really majored in James Thurber and E. B. White. I bought and read the books that they had written. I also read a lot of articles about them in the IU Library. Thurber had eye problems; so did I. White had allergy problems; so did I. They had problems with women; so did I. They wrote a book together; it was entitled *Is Sex Necessary?*

I talked with White on his birthday in 1977 and 1985. I simply called directory assistance in North Brooklin, Maine. I thanked him for his wonderful writing. He chuckled that someone would call him from Chicago.

---

[48] This count comes from Amazon, but other sources may have different numbers. Poems and essays can often be collected in different ways, making it more difficult to find an exact number of books on a given author.

PILGRIMAGE

My favorite White essay is "Freedom." In it is this sentence: "Or to an older youth, encountering for the first time a great teacher who by some chance word or mood awakens something and the youth beginning to breathe as an individual and conscious of strength in his vitals."

E. B. White died on October 1, 1985 in North Brooklin, Maine. On Saturday, August 1, 1998, I visited the farm and the town in Maine where he lived. People at the General Store told me how to get there. The folks who now own the farm were not home. So I walked the place on my own.

I saw the barn that inspired *Charlotte's Web*. There is still a rope swing in the doorway. I walked through the pastures to the shore of the cove. I looked in the window of the boathouse where White did a lot of writing. I walked on the road that led back to the house through the garden.

Then I went back to the General Store and bought a tape of what White's son, Joel, had read to his father during the last year of his life. It was several of White's essays, poems, and stories.

I walked across the street to the Library. The courtyard garden is dedicated to the memory of White and his wife, Katherine. I bought a copy of one of White's essay collections, *One Man's Meat*. White's daughter-in-law, Allene, had donated several publisher's copies for sale at the Library.

The librarian let me study the file of articles on White. She also made copies for me. I was particularly pleased to get a copy of a picture of White, in his eighties, swinging on the barn doorway rope swing. It had been part of the memorial service program.

Finishing School

In the fall of 1970, I called home from college and said, "I want to be a writer." My father replied, "It's hard to make a living as a writer. Why don't you do that as an avocation?"

The summer of 1971, I had more eye and allergy problems. So I moved back into my parents' home and commuted to Loyola University Chicago for 2 years. In the fall of 1971, instead of playing quarterback for the University of Notre Dame, I had an essay and a poem published in the Loyola literary magazine, *Cadence.*

The editor my first year had a running argument with the editor my second year about whether my essay or my poem was the best thing ever published in the magazine. I was non-committal.

When I had gathered my strength, I went back to Indiana University for my final two semesters. I lived in Alpha Epsilon Phi Sorority with seventy ladies as their houseboy.

Maryville and Ziggy Czarobski

Chicagoan Zygmont "Ziggy" Czarobski, a Mount Carmel High School and Notre Dame University Alum, was a famous Catholic athlete, an entertaining personality, and certainly one of the most important Chicagoans in Catholic charity circles. Czarobski was an all-state athlete who had made the grade at the University of Notre Dame during one of its brilliant periods on the gridiron. Czarobski was named to Grantland Rice's Football Writers Association of America (FWAA) Second Team All-American for

1947.[49] This was quite an honor considering the post war college teams were loaded with military men who had postponed their education to serve their country, just as Czarobski had done. Czarobski used his football personality, humor, and persuasion to accomplish much in life. Anyone who heard Czarobski speak, will tell you that he was a literary figure—an artist.

Czarobski had a tremendous college experience. At Notre Dame, he had a pre-war and post-war career that included three National Championships. Those championships would command good speaking engagements. Czarobski, a right tackle, had played with some of the best Notre Dame teams in history. Besides playing with legendary players, Czarobski's coach at the time was Frank Leahy, a disciplinarian who would play a leading role in Czarobski's humor. Leahy was a fine coach who became a popular sportscaster after coaching. Leahy was as disciplined as Czarobski was fun-loving.

Czarobski liked to tell audiences about the day Leahy told the team that the coach was going to start with the basics. After picking up a football, Leahy said, "Gentlemen, this is a football." Immediately Ziggy interrupted the proceeds asking Leahy to "slow it down." Teammate, John Lujack, said "Ziggy wasn't the best student Notre Dame ever had. He (Ziggy) used to tell people he was in school for two terms—Roosevelt's and Truman's."

Before coming back for one of his seasons after the War, Leahy heard that Ziggy's weight had ballooned and that he was 50 pounds overweight. Leahy sent Ziggy a note stating that the coach was not interested in the lineman at his current weight and he would have to lose

---

[49] See article online at
http://www.sportswriters.net/fwaa/awards/allamerica/alltime.pdf

50 pounds or else! There are at least three versions of what happened next, from fixing the scale, to getting a reprieve when his weight got close, to Leahy just taking it on faith that Ziggy had lost the weight. Maybe Ziggy used different versions depending upon his audience! Once called out by Leahy, Czarobski worked exceptionally hard as did others on the team. Conditioning would be one of Leahy's strong suits.

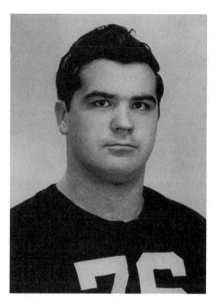

After Notre Dame, Ziggy played for the Chicago Rockets and the Chicago Hornets of the All-American Football Conference (AAFC), a professional football league that started up just after World War II. When the league folded in 1949, Ziggy's football career ended. A few AAFC teams got into the National Football League, but for many AAFC players, they were out of work. Czarobski went to work with the Illinois Secretary of State and then he began to raise funds for charity.

Czarobski was an early promoter of the Special Olympics. The Ziggy Czarobski Golf Outing recently finished its 51st Annual cycle sponsored by the Notre Dame Club of Aurora/Fox Valley and benefiting the John G. Bryan Scholarship for local students to attend Notre Dame. Czarobski also offered his services to Father John Smyth's Maryville Academy. Maryville, a residential child-care agency in Illinois, had fallen into disrepair before the legendary Father Smyth was assigned to run it. Funding was inadequate and the Archdiocese of Chicago was planning to close it. Father Smyth had other ideas and began to turn things around. He asked Czarobski to help.

Czarobski helped Smyth make the famous Maryville Academy Chuck-Wagon Barbecue one of the greatest charity events in the nation. He worked with people like Chicago Cub Gabby Hartnett; Heisman Trophy winner from Notre Dame, Johnny Lattner; Chicago Blackhawk Stan Mikita; and prominent Chicagoans business and professional people like Bill Wirtz, Tom Tully, and many others.[50]

Czarobski helped persuade many sponsoring organizations to donate the food, drinks, and other materials necessary. Czarobski was a master at persuasion and had all the needed ingredients coming onto the Maryville campus. Art Contreras, a former resident of Maryville, and John Clancy brilliantly ran the event. Many others worked to serve over 10,000 customers a year.

---

[50] See David Condon, "Polio Victim Inspired Czarobski to Football Fame," Chicago Tribune In the Wake of the News, Oct. 13, 1977, Sec. 4, page 3, viewed on Aug. 9, 2016, on http://archives.chicagotribune.com/1977/10/13/page/67/article/polio-victim-inspired-czarobski-to-football-fame.

The Maryville Academy Chuck-Wagon Barbecue brought millions of dollars to Maryville and helped the Academy expand to offer many other services and serve many more people.

Czarobski died in 1984 at the age of 61. He was inducted into the Sports Faith Hall of Fame, the College Football Hall of Fame, and the National Polish-American Hall of Fame.

Chapter 11: Guadalupe

Each December, thousands attend traditional celebrations in churches in honor of Our Lady of Guadalupe, the Patroness of the Americas. Hispanic Catholics celebrate the Virgin Mary's multiple appearances to Juan Diego Cuauhtlatoatzin, an Aztec native who converted to Catholicism.

At the time of the apparitions, the Aztecs had been defeated by the Spanish and neither people have much respect for each other. The Aztec practices include human sacrifice, which horrifies the Spanish priests. Yet, the Spanish soldiers have mistreated the natives. The situation has colored the natives view of the missionary priests—efforts to convert the natives have not gone well.

In fact, the relationship between the two groups seems to be about to come to a boil.

Juan Diego is a 57-year-old peasant making his way to Mass on the morning of December 9, 1531. Diego is an Aztec, a widower, a simple uneducated farmer and laborer, and a convert to Catholicism. He lives with his elderly uncle.

On Tepeyac Hill, Diego sees the Virgin Mary, who appears to him as a native princess—an Indian. She calms the humble man, tells him who she is in his own native language, and explains that she wants him to see the bishop and tell him she wants a church to be built on the site where she can hear the petitions of the Mexican people. She tells him:

> *Dear little son, I love you. I want you to know who I am.*
> *I am the Virgin Mary, Mother of the one true God, of Him who gives life.*
> *He is Lord and Creator of heaven and of earth. I desire that there be built a temple at this place where I want to manifest Him, make him known, give Him to all people through my love, my compassion, my help, and my protection. I truly am your merciful Mother, your Mother and the Mother of all who dwell in this land, and of all mankind, of all those who love me, of those who cry to me, and of those who seek and place their trust in me. Here I shall listen to their weeping and their sorrows.*
> *I shall take them all to my heart, and I shall cure their many sufferings,*

afflictions, and sorrows. So run now to Tenochtitlan and tell the Lord Bishop all that you have seen and heard.

Diego goes to see Bishop Juan de Zumarraga. The bishop doubts the peasant's story and wonders what he is up to. Diego leaves without convincing him. He returns to Tepeyac Hill where Our Lady appears again. Diego tells Our Lady that the bishop did not believe him. She tells him to go back to see the bishop the next day and try again.

It does not go well. The bishop tells Diego to bring him a sign. Diego tells the bishop he will return the following day. Diego sees Our Lady again and reports that the bishop has requested a sign. Our Lady tells him to come back the next day.

But when Diego goes home, he finds that his uncle, Juan Bernardino, is very ill. The illness Diego recognizes and it brings a high fever and is often fatal. Diego spends a day with his uncle and then Bernardino is near death. Diego seeks a priest, but on the road, the Lady visits him again. He explains his delayed return and he is embarrassed by his apparent lack of faith. Our Lady encourages him:

My little son. Do not be distressed and afraid. Am I not here who am your Mother? Are you not under my shadow and protection? Am I not the fountain of your joy? Are you not in the fold of my mantle, in the cradle of my arms?

Our Lady tells him his uncle will be fine and she wants him to attend to her errand. Diego remembers the bishop's requested sign. Our Lady tells him to go to the top of Tepeyac Hill and he will find flowers that he is to pick and place in his tilma (cloak) until he reaches the bishop. It's cold and it seems unlikely that flowers will be alive on the hill, but Diego finds them and gathers them in his cloak.

When Diego sees the bishop, he opens the tilma, the roses fall out, and both peasant and bishop see a beautiful image of Our Lady on the tilma. The image resembles a native princess; she is clothed in a blue cloak with stars. Under Our Lady's feet is the crescent moon, an Aztec symbol that she adapts.

At Diego's home, Our Lady appears to Juan Bernardino and his fever subsides. She tells Bernardino that she wants to be known as "Santa Maria, de Guadalupe."

The apparitions come to an end and the results are incredible. The church is built on the site outside of Mexico City. Millions of natives convert and millions make pilgrimages to see the miraculous tilma, and to honor Our Lady of Guadalupe.

On October 12, 1945, Pope Pius XII (1939–58) decreed Our Lady of Guadalupe to be "Patroness of all the Americas." Her feast day is December 12.

A 60-minute documentary, "Guadalupe: The Miracle and the Message" (in English or Spanish), was released by the Knights of Columbus in 2015. It lays out the story, history and significance of the Apparition of Our Lady of Guadalupe from the last days of the Aztec empire to the present. According to Sister Helena Burns, Catholic reviewer of film and media, "It's really not to be missed, even if you're very familiar with the story and have watched other documentaries and films on Guadalupe (as I have)."[51]

---

51 See Sister Helena's Blog, "Hell Burns," for her review of the movie at http://hellburns.blogspot.com/2015/12/movies-guadalupe-miracle-and-message-el.html#.VtShyeaoQwg .

Mexican Pilgrimages

Pilgrimages took place in Mexico even before Christianity took hold. Group pilgrimages were customary on dates related to events in the Aztec ritual calendar. And like in other parts of the world, Christian practices often build on older ones. Some of the religious activities can be traced to Spain, but others are native in origin.

In Mexico, paper wreaths are often worn as the pilgrim makes a final approach to the site; mementos are hung up at shrines once pilgrims arrive; and dances are performed in celebration. Religious theater explores the faith and it is sometimes gigantic in scale. Christmas plays, nativity scenes, and Holy Week processions are especially esteemed—floats are often used. Perhaps most important of all, Mexican religious celebrations are participatory.[52]

Maryville

The celebration at Maryville Academy's Our Lady of Guadalupe Chapel in Des Plaines, Illinois, begins with a traditional, nine-day novena. Thousands defy low temperatures and set aside sleep to commemorate the feast day as they do in other cities in the United States as well as in Mexico and Latin America. Eucharistic celebration in Our Lady of Guadalupe Chapel takes place and special Masses are said during the period.

The *Antorcha Guadalupana* or torch run takes place in many locations as well in which runners depart from their respective parishes, traversing the neighborhoods taking the message of the Virgin Mary to Catholics

---

[52] Eliot Porter and Ellen Auerbach, *Mexican Celebrations* (Albuquerque: University of New Mexico Press, 1990).

everywhere. Upon the runners' arrival at local churches, the torches are placed below images of Our Lady of Guadalupe.

Our Lady of Guadalupe's association with Juan Diego Cuauhtlatoatzin forever changed the status of Indians in the eyes of the Spanish. They went from being considered servants to fellow Christians deserving respect. Many believe Our Lady has a special love for the poor and unwanted.

Saint Viator and Dylan Full

Perched on the top of a hill in Saint Viator's home town of Lyon, France, sits the Basilica of Notre Dame de Fourvière. Like the people of Mexico City, the people of Lyon built their church to honor Our Lady. In Lyon, the Basilica offers thanks to Our Lady for her intercession that spared the town from the Black Death and other scourges.

Students at Saint Viator High School understand the traditions of faith in fighting disease. The Saint Viator High School Lacrosse Team welcomed Dylan Full, an 8-year-old brain cancer survivor from Wheaton, to the team for the 2014 season. To celebrate the addition to the team, the Lions wore gray, the color of brain cancer awareness, on the back of their helmets with the saying "full hearts." The team presented Dylan with team memorabilia and he helped out throughout the games.

Prior to Dylan's addition to the team, Coach Bill Sanford said, *"This promises to be a special event for one special boy. Our boys will be his new teammates offering friendship to him along his journey, but I know the entire community will be interested in his story and his fight against cancer."*

Dylan was battling medulloblastoma, a fast growing brain tumor. It was discovered during a routine eye exam, when his ophthalmologist observed that one of his optic nerves was swollen. He recommended an MRI. Dylan's mother, Laurie Full, said: *"The MRI revealed a tumor in the posterior fossa and right then and there our lives were forever changed."* Two days later, Dylan underwent a nine-hour surgery that removed most of the tumor, and he underwent six weeks of daily radiation to his brain and spine, followed by nine cycles of chemotherapy.

"It's been a long and challenging road," Full said.

Sanford and the team learned about Dylan through Friends of Jaclyn, whose mission it is to improve the lives of pediatric cancer patients by linking them with sports teams. *"Our participation in their organization is a way for us to live out the mission of the school,"* Sanford said. *"At the same time, Dylan will help energize and inspire our kids to work hard."* The Saint Viator High School Lacrosse Team was inducted into the Sports Faith International Hall of Fame in 2015.

But the story does not end there. Dylan has done well since the program at Saint Viator and turned his attention to raising funds for cancer though the Kids Making Change campaign. Dylan set a goal to raise $2,500 for Lurie Children's Hospital in Chicago, the hospital where he received his cancer treatment. He ended up raising $7,040 by collecting change, holding lemonade stands, and selling toys and books. Dylan, a student at Arbor View Elementary School, got his school involved in the campaign.

But the story does not end there. Popular Radio hosts from THE MIX, FM 101.9, Eric and Kathy asked Dylan to come on their Radiothon to raise more money for the hospital. Dylan's funds launched a matching gift challenge hour. Dylan spoke on the show and to callers. The overall event raised $1.4 million with over $43,000 coming in during Dylan's hour alone.

Mount Notre Dame High School

The Mount Notre Dame High School Girls Volleyball Team of Cincinnati won eight State Championships as we go to press in 2016. According to Athletic Director, Mark Schenkel, *"service to others is part of the culture—students build positive relationships with the community. Students are challenged to develop a sense of social responsibility and a solid understanding of Catholic social teaching so that they can advocate justice."*

Members of the volleyball team excel in service; both coaches and players are people of strong Catholic faith, values, and tradition. Like Saint Julie Billiart, foundress of the Sisters of the Notre Dame de Namur, they proclaim the goodness of God by their lives and how they serve those on the margins of society.

All players on the team play a key role in their success year in and year out. Practice is high energy and high level. According to Schenkel, they succeed *"through hard work, determination, belief, selflessness, and an incredible team attitude."* In six seasons, current Head Coach Joe Burke's teams have a 143-24 record and four State Championships. Rachael Adams from the 2008 Class was a member of the 2016 U.S. Olympic Women's Volleyball team that won a bronze medal.

Saint Mary's Doing It Well

Sports Faith International inducted into its Hall of Fame the girls Saint Mary's High School Basketball Team of Stockton, California, for their outstanding record, service to the community, and faith. The team continues its remarkable streak of success. The team has eight State Championships as we go to press.

But the team is about more than basketball. Saint Mary's participates in helping out grammar schools, hospitals, and other non-profit community agencies—they pitch in and provide food for the hungry at Thanksgiving and toys for needy children at Christmas. They attend Mass as a group, open every practice with a prayer, and participate in a morning "direction of intention" to start each day. The girls live out the saying of the Oblates of Saint Francis de Sales: "Be who you are and be that well."

My Best Hit

In the spring
Of 1964,
I was
On the freshman baseball team
At Notre Dame High School.
On a Friday afternoon,
We had a game
At Ridgewood High School.
I was a substitute catcher.
In the top
Of the last inning,
I hit a home run
To left center
Onto the tennis courts.
The coach said it
Would have gone out
Of Wrigley Field.
We won.
After the game,

The coach got
On the team bus
And said,
"Because of the way
That we won the game,
There's no practice tomorrow."
That was very fortunate
For me
Because
I had Saturday detention.
　　—Patrick McCaskey

Rough Times

I have sympathy for anyone who is in high school. I remember what it was like. High School was rough. I was on the freshman football team. I was calling out the signals as quarterback one game and my voice cracked. I said, "Ready" (in a deep voice). "Set" (in a high voice). The guy playing right end for our team fell on the ground laughing. I had to call time out to give a chance to recover. The delay killed our momentum on that drive. We only won the game, 50-0.

I was on the freshman basketball team. I didn't go to the Bears' 1963 NFL Championship game because I had practice. When I used that as an illustration to my sons as to how dedicated they should be to their teams, they said, "Dad, you made a mistake."

I was on the freshman baseball team. I was late for practice one day because of detention. I didn't take the time to put on a protective cup before I caught batting practice. A foul ball made me wish I had.

I was on the sophomore football team. I started at end, halfback, fullback, and kicker. Then I didn't have to call signals.

PILGRIMAGE

I was on the sophomore basketball team. I didn't start against Glenbrook North, but I fouled out before the half.

I didn't make the sophomore baseball team. I'm not bitter.

At the start of my junior football season, I failed the physical because of a hernia. Remember that foul ball? My voice cracked that day.

Instead of going out for basketball, I worked out with the swimming team. I nearly drowned every practice.

When I went out for track, the coach said that I ran like a football player. I took that as a compliment. I rode my bike 25 miles from Des Plaines to Wheaton to see Louise Raymond. She wasn't home. I was fifth in the conference mile. We won the conference meet.

When I was a senior, I was quarterback on defense and offense. My voice did not crack. We won every game by an average of 29 points. I threw some interceptions at away games and I'm still working off Father Corcoran's penance. Pete Newell and I were *Catholic New World* All-Americans.

Owen Bauler and I were track co-captains. We won the conference meet by 29 points. He was most valuable. I was most improved. He still has school sprint records. My distance records were quickly broken.

Scherpenheuvel Basilica

Chapter 12: Scherpenheuvel

A short distance from Diest, Belgium, on a high hill, stands the Sanctuary or Shrine of Our Lady of Montaigu also called Our Lady of Scherpenheuvel.[53] The shrine on the "sharp" hill, Scherpenheuvel, began its history centuries ago. A statue of Mary was hung in an old oak tree on the site and people came to visit the site in 1304. Some suggest that perhaps the tree itself had importance with the Druids. Others suggest that tree's cross-like shape may have been the reason that pilgrims were attracted to the site. While the site was developing a following, the Reformation and Counter Reformation were happening and many political battles were being fought out.

---

[53] See home page of Our Lady of Scherpenheuvel at http://www.scherpenheuvel.be/en. The different names for the Shine are derived from the French and Dutch languages spoken in Belgium.

PILGRIMAGE

A little shepherd boy tried to take away the small statue when it had fallen from its perch in the tree, but he was paralyzed on the spot until his master found him and replaced the statue in the tree. Pilgrims visited the Scherpenheuvel Shrine and Protestants who were militantly against icons looted the region and some believe they stole the statue in 1587. A similar statue was obtained in nearby Diest that some believe was the original brought to safety. This same statue is revered now.

Cures were attributed at the site through the intercession by the Virgin and the number of pilgrims increased. People believed in the healing forces of the oak and they cut pieces of the tree as a relic effectively destroying the tree.[54] A wooden chapel was built. Spanish Archduke Albrecht and Archduchess Isabella governed the region and visited regularly. In 1604 they replaced the wooden chapel by a stone one.

Albrecht and Isabella planned to build a large church at the site of the old oak tree. In 1609 the construction of the Basilica in Scherpenheuvel, as a product of the Counter-Reformation was started and completed in 1627.[55] Archduke Albrecht who died in 1621 did not live to witness the consecration of the Basilica; Isabella was present. After the consecration, Isabella put her jewels at the foot of the altar and that gesture is today a popular custom of pilgrims who offer money and jewelry at the shrine.

---

[54] Some suggest that the Catholic Church favored the destruction of the tree. The tree promoted a pre-Christian importance in nature as a deity. The Church promotes devotion to Mary as an intercessor. The Church extols the importance of icons, but only as a sacred symbol.

[55] The Counter Reformation was a movement within the Roman Catholic Church for reform.

In 1624, an oratory (a large complex of buildings with a courtyard) was built beside the church and in 1660 the cloister was connected to the church. Until 1797, the Oratory Fathers offered church services as the French Revolution was going on, but the day before Christmas 1797, they were expelled and deported to South America.[56]

The miraculous statue was installed in 1850 in a silver tabernacle. Many improvements have been made to the church and in 1922 the church received the honorary title of basilica.

The church's main altar and six side altars have altarpieces by artist Theodoor van Loon that depict scenes from the life of the Blessed Virgin: the Immaculate Conception, Mary's Birth, Mary's Presentation, the Annunciation, the Visitation, the Presentation of Jesus at the Temple, and the Assumption.

Saint John Berchmans

Saint John Berchmans, patron saint of altar boys, was born in Diest, Belgium, on March 13, 1599. The son of a shoemaker, he wanted to be a priest at an early age. Berchmans made pilgrimages to the Our Lady of Montaigu Shrine where a Basilica now stands. Although unfinished in his lifetime, the shrine was a place of powerful prayer for him.

Berchmans spent much of his time at church saying the rosary, and early in the day, he often served as an altar boy for Mass. His father, Charles Berchmans,

---

[56] Belgium was part of the Spanish Netherland and would come under control of the Spanish, the Austrians and the French during this tumultuous times. During the French Revolution, the church properties were seized, religious property was confiscated and destroyed.

agreed to send John to Mechlin, where he lived in the household of Canon John Froymont and was able to continue his studies in return for his domestic services. A gifted student, he later enrolled at the Jesuit College at Malines in 1615 and became a Jesuit novice a year later. He was sent to the College of the Society at Antwerp, where he stayed for two months and then went on to Rome in 1618 to continue his studies. After a philosophical discussion at the Greek College in Rome, Saint John Berchmans became ill with inflamed lungs. His condition never improved and he died there on August 23, 1621, before completing his studies for the priesthood. His feast day is November 23.

Like the Little Flower, Saint John Berchmans did little things very well and people loved him. He was devoted to the Mother of God. As a young boy, he watched his own mother suffer through a terminal illness. He spoke of the possibility of his own martyrdom. A religious war waged between Protestants and Catholics at the time in the area. Those around Saint John Berchmans, knew he was devout. His piety and humility struck people every stop that he made along the way in his very short life. Many people felt a closeness to God when around him.

A large crowd was there to see his remains before he was buried in the Church of Saint Ignatius. The same year, Pope Gregory XV (1621-1623) was petitioned to gather information with the intent of beatification. On the 28th of May, 1865, during the Pontificate of Pius IX (1846-1878), the Decree of Beatification was solemnly pronounced in Saint Peter's. On the 22nd of January, 1888, Pope Leo XIII (1878-1903) issued the Bull of Canonization.

Saint John Berchmans Parish and School

In 2016, I visited Saint John Berchmans School at the invitation of Father Wayne F. Watts, the Pastor, and Jennifer Cortez, the Director of Stewardship and Liturgy. The church and school are located in the Logan Square community in Chicago. The school has served the community for over 100 years and remains vibrant to humbly serve others. Saint John Berchmans School continues to provide Christian based quality education to the families of Logan Square and nearby communities. The school helps "nourish both the body and the soul of our community." It operates like many Catholic Schools today in a diverse learning atmosphere, with faith-focused teaching that "gives students the ability to learn without distractions and dream without limits."

Gavin Provost: Living Witness

Gavin Provost is a determined young man who was born with spina bifida, a birth defect that paralyzed his legs, caused neurological damage, and gave rise to 11 operations. Gavin has never stopped challenging himself athletically and spiritually. He is a living witness of one of the Catholic Faith's most important teachings: Our frustrations and crosses, by God's grace, have the power to become our greatest victory. They are the gifts God gives us to bring His Kingdom to life here on earth, and fulfill a unique part of His plan. A plan only we can do and only if we say "yes."

Gavin lives with exemplary courage, perseverance, and faith. Triumphing over his initial fears and failures, he refused to allow the paralysis in his legs to prevent him from swimming on three different teams since the age of nine. He won the "Most Inspirational Swimmer Award." He went on to use his swimming talent to help the sick, swimming 50 laps and raising $1,800 in a swim-a-thon for the Evan Halford Foundation that provides financial assistance to families who have a child with cancer. A great love for football led Gavin to serve Saint Joseph High School in South Bend, where he enjoyed a 2-year stint as manager of the football team. Gavin knew as a freshman that he must challenge himself spiritually. He became a Catholic and his parents followed. He taught seventh graders CCD (Confraternity of Christian Doctrine), and worked with youth groups. Gavin Provost was the recipient of Sports Faith International's Spirit of Saint Paul Award.

Mark Philippi

Mark Philippi is a nationally recognized Strength and Conditioning Coach and a strength athlete. In powerlifting, Mark won the World Drug Free Powerlifting Championships in 1996. Mark won America's Strongest Man in 1997. He has appeared on the World's Strongest Man television show seven times and competed in over 100 international strongman competitions.

Currently Mark and his wife, Tracey, run Philippi Sports Institute in Las Vegas, Nevada, a facility that offers support services in strength training, nutrition, rehabilitation, and sports therapy to meet the needs of the modern athlete. Mark offers his services as a strength and conditioning coach. Tracey is Director of Sports Nutrition and Functional Medicine. Mark and his staff have trained thousands of athletes including many in professional sports. As a strength and conditioning celebrity, Mark has been featured on many TV shows and in magazines throughout his career. Mark was the Director of Strength and Conditioning at the University of Nevada, Las Vegas (UNLV) for 15 years.

Marc (spelled with a "c") Philippi is Mark and Tracey Philippi's eldest son. Marc is a UNLV fullback who has loved football over all other sports. Marc Philippi and his parents are devout Catholics. Like all his siblings, Marc was home-schooled by his mother. At home, he received a solid Catholic education and avoided some bad influences that according to his father are sometimes found in Las Vegas more than most other places. Homeschooling seemed to be a good solution to several problems, including what was originally overcrowding in the schools.

Marc looks up to his father and mother not just for their enthusiasm and accomplishment in sports, but because of their faith. He frequents the Newman Center during the week and is back with family on weekends. For the family, raising good kids in a Vegas culture can be challenging, but the Philippis have managed by keeping their kids from the excesses and promoting their Catholic values.

Reading and Writing

When I was a student at Saint Mary's School in Des Plaines, the City of Destiny, I was in the Bluebirds Reading Group. I used to enjoy getting up in front of my classmates and reading to them.

When I was a student at Notre Dame High School in Niles, the All American City, my writing teacher, Father Sandonato, said to me, "McCaskey, you have a unique writing talent. You should develop it."

I replied, "Father, I have to get to practice."

When I was a student at Cheshire Academy in Connecticut, the Constitution State, I read an essay that wasn't even assigned. It was "University Days" by James Thurber. Then I read every Thurber book in the Cheshire Public Library.

When I was a student at Indiana University in Bloomington, the hometown of Hoagy Carmichael, I was an English major because I wanted to be a writer. I really majored in James Thurber and E. B. White. I read all of their books in the wonderful IU Library.

Fromm to McCaskey to White

Love is an act of faith.
Writing is an act of love.
Writing is an act of faith.
—Patrick McCaskey

Declared a Martyr?

In 1964, when I was a high school sophomore, I had hairline fractures in both hands during the preseason football practices. The varsity football coach, Fran Willett, said to me, "You don't run with your hands. Stay in shape."

In 1967, my aunt Julie, declared a McCaskey Martyr Contest. Everyone had the opportunity to state their case. Later, my sister Mary, was the clear winner because she said, "I didn't even know there was a contest."

On Saturday, September 26, 2015, I went to 8:00 a.m. Mass at Saint Mary's Lake Forest. During Mass, some church concrete steps were painted.

After Mass, I had a church bulletin and my "Magnificat" booklet in my left hand. I slipped coming down the concrete stairs that were newly painted and still wet. My feet went out from under me and I bounced down a couple of steps. My left hand was bruised and my right hand was lacerated.

Father Grzesik of Saint Mary's had said the Mass. He was called out of Confession. He gave me a blessing that was not the Last Rites. He said that the Church insurance would cover any costs. A Good Samaritan drove my car to the Lake Forest Hospital.

The Lake Forest Fire Department Ambulance took me to the Lake Forest Hospital Emergency Room. My hands were x-rayed. My right hand received eight stitches. Yogi Berra was number 8.

The doctor is a Packers' fan. I told him don't be discouraged. Some of the greatest Christians started out as atheists. Jesus forgave the good thief. All he has to do is repent.

The Packers are doing very well for an expansion team. The Packers have 13 championships. The Bears have nine. This is disconcerting.

Joan McHugh of Sports Faith International had been at the Mass. She called my wife, Gretchen, who has a masters' degree in nursing. I have a First Aid merit badge. It was good to get other opinions.

Doug Plank used to say, "I'm cured; I just have some of the symptoms."

Father Grzesik also came to the hospital and repeatedly said that the Church insurance would cover any costs. I hope that the painter goes to Confession. I wonder if the Church will declare me a martyr.

Chapter 13: The Popes

I have gone on "pilgrimages" to see two Popes.

Pope Francis

On Friday, September 18, 2015, I received a phone call from Angela Tomlinson of Sports Faith International. She said that Lake County Sheriff Mark Curran had access to two tickets to the Pope's address to Congress. Was I interested? Yes I was.

I offered one ticket to Ray McKenna of Catholic Athletes for Christ because he had given me a ticket to Pope Benedict XVI at the White House in 2008. Ray accepted and he offered me a ticket to the Papal Mass. Was I interested? Yes I was.

Nancy Sheahan of Frosch Travel arranged for me to be on United Airlines flights. She also arranged for me to stay at the Willard Hotel, 1401 Pennsylvania Avenue, NW.

On Tuesday, September 22, Ray McKenna and his wife met me at Washington Reagan National Airport. They had left their children at home to say the rosary. They gave me a ride to the Willard Hotel.

Ray explained that Abraham Lincoln had stayed there while the White House was being renovated. People who had business with the President waited in the hotel lobby. That's how we got the term lobbyist.

Ray had a luncheon for Craig Stammen who was on the disabled list for the Washington Nationals. Craig played football, basketball, and baseball at Versailles High School which is near North Star, Ohio. In 2002, he was Academic All-Ohio in baseball. Then he pitched for the University of Dayton where he majored in entrepreneurship and business management. He is a college graduate.

In 2005, Craig began speaking about his Catholic faith. From a 2013 interview in National Catholic Register, we know that "When Stammen pitches, he knows that once the ball is out of his hands, everything else is out of his hands as well. More importantly, though, he realizes everything is in the hands of a God in whom he lives and moves and has his being..."

Craig said, "The entire village of North Star is Catholic, so even though I went to a public school, it was de facto a Catholic one. When people outside of North Star ask if I went to a Catholic school, the answer is, 'Well, no, but yes...'

"I used to play for my teammates and school, which was a good thing, but now I play for God, which is an even better thing. It's a much broader-minded way of seeing things, and it takes a lot of the pressure off you. It opens you up to the reality that, while baseball is fun, you can't really enjoy it to the fullest or play it to the best of your abilities without recognizing the God who made it all possible in the first place."

After lunch, we went to the Basilica of the National Shrine of the Immaculate Conception on the campus of Catholic University of America. The security checkpoint was very crowded and very slow. There were some people in the crowd who weren't living the gospel. Then some other people said the rosary out loud.

Two ladies who didn't have tickets asked me how I got mine. I explained that my Confirmation name was Paul. Paul said that he was the foremost sinner. Since I had chosen the name of the foremost sinner, I received a ticket.

The Canonization Mass of Blessed Junipero Serra was in English and several other languages. The highlight of the trip was receiving Communion at a Papal Mass. When we receive Communion, we become more like Jesus. When we eat potato chips, we do not become more like Chip Hilton.[57]

After Mass, I talked with Mike Bidwill, the Arizona Cardinals' President. He had gone to law school at Catholic University of America. He also said that Dan and Pat Rooney of the Pittsburgh Steelers had been at the Mass.

Then I talked with Brother John Yep from Illinois, the Land of Lincoln. He is in seminary in Los Angeles because he wants to be a priest in the media.

---

[57] Fiction sports hero in popular book series originally published in late 1940s and 1950s by author Clair Bee. Revised editions published in the 1990s.

On Thursday, September 24, Ray and I went to hear and see the Pope address Congress. Ray recalled that when Bishop Sheen addressed a group where many people had been acknowledged, he began by saying "Fellow sinners. Have I left anyone out?"

Pope Francis did not use Bishop Sheen's quote. Pope Francis acknowledged four great United States citizens: Abraham Lincoln, Martin Luther King Junior, Dorothy Day, and Thomas Merton. Pope Francis did not use my Martin Luther King Junior joke.

True or false: Martin Luther King Junior played quarterback for Morehouse College: True.

True or false: His team was constantly penalized for delay of game because he kept making speeches in the huddle: False.

After the Pope had waved to everyone, Ray and I visited with Illinois Tenth District Congressman Bob Dold in his office. Bob had played quarterback for New Trier High School. He had also wrestled and played lacrosse. We got to meet several members of Bob's family.

Pope Francis was surprised to have been elected Pope. Perhaps he said, "Shut my mouth and call me Francis." Maybe I got to hear and see the Pope because I was born at Saint Francis Hospital.

If Charlotte had written in her web about Pope Francis, she could very well have written: "Some Pope," "Terrific," "Radiant," and "Humble."

Pope Benedict XVI

I received a call from Ray McKenna who invited me to help President George W. Bush and Mrs. Bush welcome His Holiness Pope Benedict XVI to the White House South Lawn on Wednesday, April 16, 2008. People stood as far away as the Washington Monument and the Jefferson Memorial.

President Bush expressed his thoughts on America and its faith. He told Pope Benedict that in America you'll find a nation of prayer, compassion, and one that welcomes the role of faith.

Pope Benedict XVI spoke about a moral order based on the dominion of God. Americans drew upon this when they proclaimed the "self-evident truth" that all men are created equal and endowed with unalienable rights grounded in the laws of nature and of nature's God.

The preservation of freedom calls for virtue, self-discipline, sacrifice, and responsibility towards the less fortunate. Faith sheds new light on all things. Faith gives us the strength to respond to our high calling.

On Thursday morning, April 17, we went to Nationals Park for Mass with the Pope. In his homily, the Pope said:

I have come to proclaim anew, as Peter proclaimed on the day of Pentecost, that Jesus Christ is Lord and Messiah, risen from the dead, seated in glory at the right hand of the Father, and established as judge of the living and the dead. I have come to repeat the Apostle's urgent call to conversion and the forgiveness of sins, and to implore from the Lord a new outpouring of the Holy Spirit upon the Church in this country.

The whole experience was edifying, encouraging, exhilarating, and inspirational.

Lou Gehrig

Henry Louis "Lou" Gehrig was an interesting man for a number of odd reasons. First, he came along in the Yankees historic days when Babe Ruth was the center of attention in baseball. When Ruth was finished playing, another tremendous star took his place in the sun, Joe DiMaggio.

Gehrig played for the longest streak in baseball, 2,130 baseball games over a 14 year period until his streak was surpassed by Cal Ripken Jr. in 1995. Called the Iron Horse for his durability, Gehrig piled up superstar statistics that were overshadowed by Ruth's and then he was snuffed out by a horrible disease, amyotrophic lateral sclerosis (ALS), also known as Lou Gehrig's disease for many years.

While Ruth was a party-hardy guy in his youth and DiMaggio was famous for dating showgirls and hanging out in nightclubs, Gehrig was devoted to his mother and his wife. Gehrig had a big boned football player physique while chubby Ruth exuded power. DiMaggio was simply the most graceful player of his day.

Gehrig often appeared uncoordinated as a young ballplayer. Miller Huggins, his early coach with the Yankees, had confidence in Gehrig when others wondered if he would ever amount to much. After extensive training and a spell in the minors, his fielding improved.

Gehrig had grown up poor in New York. His mother Christina worked as a domestic among other low-paying jobs. His father Heinrich had some metal-working skills and had many odd jobs. Both Christina and Heinrich had emigrated from Germany leaving poor situations and looking for better. They found tragedy and difficult living conditions until their son rescued them from poverty. Two Gehrig children died while infants and one at birth. Lou's mother was determined to keep Lou, her remaining child healthy. Christina was built sturdy and strong. She filled her waking hours with work. Wealthy clients were nearby and small jobs could be found.

Heinrich's work habits were lacking. Lou would grow up with an appreciation for his mother and what she went through to raise him. Both Gehrig's parents were Lutherans.

As a young boy, Gehrig looked chubby, but he was exceptionally strong. There was a sense of decency in the young man's behavior while others around him failed. Gehrig was a strong athlete who never took aggression out on others. He was a patient player, but one day he had enough of the Detroit Tigers' star Ty Cobb who seemed to have it out for Gehrig. Gehrig went after Cobb in the dugout.[58] Gehrig banged his head and was kept away from Cobb by others. Cobb decided to cool his anti-Gehrig rhetoric after that. Another player, Bucky Harris had purposefully spiked Gehrig going to first base and Gehrig's response was a muffed play and a simple look of disbelief. Eventually, an apology from Harris was rendered. Gehrig's innocence was disarming. He was one of the best men in baseball.

Gehrig's parents, Christina and Heinrich, had worked at Sigma Nu Fraternity at Columbia University when Lou was young. At Columbia, his mother worked in the cafeteria and his father did odd jobs. A few years later when the family had moved, Gehrig was playing baseball and football at the High School of Commerce. Gehrig and his pals were familiar with the New York Giants who played in the Polo Grounds and the Highlanders, who would become the Yankees, who played at Hilltop Park.

Gehrig gained national attention on June 26, 1920, when the city of Chicago sponsored a baseball game between the New York City high school champions, the

---

[58] Jack Sher, "Lou Gehrig: The Man and the Legend," *Sport Magazine*, October 1951.

High School of Commerce, and the Chicago champion, Lane Tech High School. The game was at Cubs Park—later to be called Wrigley Field. In the top of the ninth inning, with Commerce leading, 8–6, Gehrig came to the plate with the bases loaded. He bashed the first pitch over the wall for a grand slam. Gehrig's "major league" hit made the sports pages of the *Chicago Tribune*: "Gehrig's blow would have made any big leaguer proud, yet it was walloped by a boy who hasn't yet started to shave."[59]

Gehrig was scouted by the athletic director of Columbia who had met the parents when they worked at the school. A scholarship in football followed. Gehrig would play baseball and football at Columbia. Gehrig got roped into playing professional baseball under fictitious names for the Hartford Senators of the Class A Eastern League in the 1921 season. He ended up being disqualified at Columbia for one season.

When Gehrig did play for Columbia, scouts took notice. Like Babe Ruth, Gehrig was both a great hitter and a pitcher of some note. In one game, Gehrig struck out 17 batters, setting a school record that remains at Columbia.[60] And as for hitting, people still talk about where some of Gehrig's home runs landed.

Gehrig and the Yankees

Gehrig left Columbia after a couple years and signed with the Yankees. Gehrig sent almost every penny

[59] James Lincoln Ray, "Lou Gehrig," SABR Baseball Biography Project, viewed at http://sabr.org/bioproj/person/ccdffd4c on November 24, 2015.
[60] James Lincoln Ray, "Lou Gehrig," SABR Baseball Biography Project, viewed at http://sabr.org/bioproj/person/ccdffd4c on November 24, 2015.

home and continued to support his family. One year, just at the start of the season, he used his check to pay for an operation for his father. Gehrig was broke and hungry! When others noticed his dilemma, funds were advanced to him. His early Yankee years were devoted to improving his parents living conditions.

Gehrig was quiet and shy, but he still hankered for fans' adulation. He never quite had it until his career was coming to an end. Playing in 17 seasons (1923-1939), Gehrig had eight 200-plus hit seasons and the Yankees won seven pennants and six World Series. He ended atop the American League in runs four times, home runs three times, runs-batted in five times, on-base percentage five times, and batting average once. Seven times, he finished among the league's top three hitters. For 13-straight seasons, Gehrig scored over 100 runs and drove in over 100 runs. His 23 grand slams was a major league record. In 1931, he set the AL single-season RBI mark with 184. In 1934 Gehrig achieved a triple-crown season: batting .363, hitting 49 homeruns, and driving in 165 runs.

For the first seven seasons of All-Star play from 1933-1939, he was the American League first baseman. And yet, according to baseball writer Jack Sher, Gehrig "always seemed to rise to his greatest heights at the precise time when it would be least noticed.[61] Gehrig's World Series average was .361 and he batted in the most runs in a World Series at 35. He had the most homers in three consecutive series games, 4, and he hit the most home runs in the series, 10. But that was not enough. The day Ruth famously called his shot (predicted he would homer) against the Cubs in the World Series of 1932,

---

61 Jack Sher, "Lou Gehrig: The Man and the Legend," Sport Magazine, October 1951.

Gehrig kept up with Ruth and hit two homers that day just as the "Babe" had done.[62]

Gehrig was known by teammates as Buster. On the day he hit four consecutive home runs in one outing, New York Giants Hall of Fame Coach John McGraw retired that day and got all the headlines. [63] And so went the career of Lou Gehrig...

Gehrig fell in love with a vivacious young women whom he had met in Chicago, Eleanor Twitchell. Twitchell's father was a successful Chicago business owner who lost most everything in the stock market crash. Unlike Gehrig, Twitchell was outgoing. It took him a long time to propose, but she helped him get through it. Married at 30, Gehrig got sick 5 years later and Eleanor supported him throughout. When Gehrig became ill, he finally felt the affection of fans. He finally knew that he was loved. Gehrig's consecutive games streak came to an end on May 2, 1939, when he removed himself from the lineup after a dismal start caused by his mysterious neuromuscular disease, amyotrophic lateral sclerosis.

Gehrig was the Yankee captain from 1935 until his death in 1941. The Baseball Writers Association of America voted him the greatest first baseman of all time in 1969. On the 50th anniversary of the end of his streak in 1989, a United States commemorative postage stamp depicting Gehrig was issued. In 1999, he was the leading vote-getter for Major League Baseball's All-Century Team.

---

62 Ruth was seen pointing towards center field stands to show the Cubs where he was going to hit the ball.

63 Jack Sher, "Lou Gehrig: The Man and the Legend," Sport Magazine, October 1951.

PILGRIMAGE

On June 21, 1939, the Yankees issued an announcement that Gehrig was retiring and that July 4 would be Lou Gehrig Appreciation Day. The ceremony took place between games of a doubleheader between the Yankees and the Washington Senators. Notable members of the great 1927 Murderers' Row team showed up and many New York dignitaries. After preliminary speeches, Gehrig took the microphone after encouragement from current Yankees manager, Joe McCarthy.[64] To the crowd, he said:

Fans, for the past two weeks you have been reading about a bad break. Today, I consider myself the luckiest man on the face of the earth...

Gehrig's farewell speech is thought to be one of the best sports moments of all time. It was also used in a movie made on Gehrig's life called "Pride of the Yankees."

Gehrig, the quiet clumsy guy with a great swing and an even greater character, was finished with baseball. Gehrig's career statistics were notable: .340 batting average, 493 home runs, 1,995 RBIs, 534 doubles, 163 triples and a .632 slugging percentage. He clung to hope against a disease that still has no cure. His wife Eleanor kept a positive outlook in the Gehrig home and he had many visitors in the two years he lived after his retirement from baseball. He died on June 2, 1941. Gehrig's funeral was at Christ Church Riverdale close to where he and his wife lived in the final months of his life.

Today, many people have taken part in a fund-raising effort to fight amyotrophic lateral sclerosis called the ALS Ice Bucket Challenge that began in the summer of 2014 and became the world's largest global social

---

[64] J.D. Thorne, *The 10 Commandments of Baseball*, (Crystal Lake, IL: Sporting Chance Press, 2009) 44.

media phenomenon. Millions of people uploaded their challenge videos and they have been watched by 440 million people a total of 10 billion times.[65]

Bushing-Oetting Reunion

A few years ago we had a family reunion for my grandmother Min's family. Like Lou Gehrig, my grandmother was of German descent. With my appreciation to Lou Gehrig, I penned the following:

When I think about whether or not being the coordinator of this family reunion is a bad break, I rewrite Lou Gehrig's Speech.

Family, for the past three months you have been hearing from me about this family reunion.

I have been in this family for sixty-two years, and I have never received anything but kindness and encouragement from you. Look at yourselves. Which of you wouldn't consider it the highlight of your life just to be in this family for even one day?

Sure I'm lucky.

Who wouldn't consider it an honor to have known Grandma Min? Also, the builder of football's greatest charter franchise, Grandpa George? To have spent time with that wonderful lady, Aunt Pat. To have spent years with that man of integrity, honesty, and decency, Uncle Mugs.

Sure I'm lucky.

When the Green Bay Packers, a team you really enjoy defeating, and vice versa, doesn't wreck this family

---

[65] ALS Association "FAQ on Ice Bucket Challenge," viewed at http://www.alsa.org/about-us/ice-bucket-challenge-faq.html on November 30, 2015.

reunion—that's something. When the Chicago Hilton & Towers hosts this family reunion, that's something.

When Janice Cole and George Oetting help you with this family reunion—that's something.

When you have a father and mother who work all their lives so that you can have an education and build your body—it's a blessing.

When you have a wife who has been a tower of strength and shown more courage than you dreamed existed—that's the finest I know.

Some people say that I've had a bad break. Yet today I consider myself the luckiest man on the face of the earth.

Chapter 14: Mature Bears

I have written and spoken much about players and coaches over my 40+ year association with the Bears. I attend funerals of Bears, often in places far away. These pilgrimages give me an opportunity to pay my respects to a soul who has gone on to glory. All of my speaking engagements allow me to share memories of people who made great contributions to our team.

Doug Atkins's Funeral, January 2, 2016

Doug Atkins was one of the most popular Bears player and certainly a gifted athlete. At Doug Atkins's funeral, I recalled my father Ed McCaskey's presenting the great athlete for induction into the Pro Football Hall of Fame on August 7, 1982.

Doug Atkins was a great football player. Anyone who ever played with him, anyone who played against him, anyone who ever coached him, and anyone who ever saw him play will attest to the truth of that statement.

Doug played his college football at the University of Tennessee. Actually, he went there on a basketball scholarship but when the head football coach, General Bob Neyland, saw him playing basketball, he marveled at Doug's agility and size and soon persuaded him to play football for the Volunteers. In his senior year he was an All-American tackle. The Cleveland Browns thought enough of him to make him their first pick in the 1953 draft.

George Halas said that one of his finest trades was when he acquired Doug Atkins in 1955. The stories about Doug and his practice routines are numerous and funny. Doug believed that football should be played on Sunday afternoon. He didn't like to practice. Throughout his career with the Bears, he played with the characteristic zest of a rookie. He was awesome, and for a man his size he had great speed. His ability to leap over opposing linemen poised to block him from quarterbacks was an important factor in winning All-NFL honors in 1960, 1961, and 1963. Doug played in eight Pro Bowl games.

Doug was a Sunday football player, but he was not above fun even on Sunday. During the '50s, two of Doug's great buddies were Fred Williams and Bill George. When the Bears traveled for road games, they took with them one dozen footballs in a canvas sack. Coach Halas noticed that we were losing a lot of balls on the road trips, so he appointed Bill George in charge of the ball-retrieving teams and Fred Williams as the assistant. If we finished the season with the same number of balls as we started that year, each was to get $100, and for every extra ball there would be a $5 bonus. The Bears never came home with less than 12 balls and usually with 13 or 14. I can tell you how we got one extra ball on every road game.

As you know, the adrenalin is pretty high just before the kickoff. Bill George was our captain and he would go out to meet the opposing captain and the officials for the coin toss. The referee always carried a football to this little ceremony.

No matter who won the toss, Bill George would say to the referee, "Mr. Referee, I'm the captain—may I have the ball please." Invariably the referee would hand Bill the ball and he would trot to the Bear bench and hand it to Doug. If the referee or anyone else suggested he surrender the ball, he would clamp both hands on it and say, "Our captain, Bill George, told me to handle this ball." *Eventually the official would shrug, go to the home-team bench, and get another ball to start the game. I don't know if Doug ever shared in the bonus money, but if he didn't, I'm sure he will want to talk to Bill George and Fred Williams.*

Because of my proximity to all things involving the Bears, my heroes were always Bears, and Doug was certainly one of them. I remember one time standing next to the great Clark Shaughnessy during a practice session at Saint Joseph's College at Rensselaer, Indiana. He said to me, "Now, I'll show you who the great athletes are." He blew his whistle and told the defensive squad to use a football and play volleyball utilizing the goal post. As we stood there watching these giants batting the football back and forth, Clark said to me, "The greatest athlete out there is Doug Atkins."

Doug played two years for the Cleveland Browns and 12 years for the Chicago Bears and finished his career with three years as a New Orleans Saint. Weeb Ewbank, who signed him to his first NFL contract, said of Doug, "Atkins was the most magnificent physical specimen I had ever seen."

Throughout his career Doug always felt his primary responsibility was making life miserable for opposing quarterbacks. Despite his unusual approach to practice, he always insisted that his teammates be ready by Sunday—and on Sunday, he excelled.

The stories about him are legend. As recently as last night, Doug said to me, "I don't know why they talk about these things. I don't drink; I don't smoke.

Anybody's wife or sister is safe with me. I just try to get along."

For 17 years he got along in the NFL. Throughout his 12 years with the Bears, he and Coach Halas argued constantly, but they usually argued about football strategy. Usually, unfortunately for Coach Halas, Doug sometimes felt that it was important that he use the telephone to discuss matters with the coach, and all too often his timing was inopportune. He didn't hesitate to call the coach at 3:00 in the morning to tell him he didn't think a play would work.

Despite their flare-ups, they had great respect for each other, and Doug remains one Bear from that era who was never fined.

In a recent TV interview, Coach Halas was asked what he thought about Doug. We have it on tape so I know that it is true. Coach Halas said, "Doug Atkins was the greatest defensive end I ever saw."

It was a privilege and pleasure for my father to present for induction into the Professional Football Hall of Fame, George Halas's greatest defensive end—a true football hero, Mr. Doug Atkins.

Ted Karras's Funeral, January 30, 2016

Here are my thoughts on Ted Karras at his funeral:

Just before the 1960 season, offensive guard Ted Karras, who had played for the Pittsburgh Steelers in 1958 and 1959, got a call from a secretary in the Bears' front office to set up a meeting with my grandfather, George Halas. Grandpa wanted to sign Karras; he had $7,000 and a $500 bonus waiting for him.

But Karras hesitated. He told Grandpa the Cardinals had offered him $8,000.

Grandpa asked, "Who would you rather play for? The Cardinals at $8,000 or the Bears at $7,500?"

The Cardinals had just suffered through a 2–10 season in 1959 and could not compete with the Bears in Chicago, so their owner, Violet Bidwill, decided to move the team to Saint Louis in 1960.

Karras decided an extra $500 wasn't worth moving and playing for a team that was struggling. He signed with the Bears and ended up being the starting left guard on the Bears' 1963 Championship Team.

In 1983, Ted was invited to speak at a 20-year reunion of the 1963 Championship Team. He was one of three brothers who were all outstanding college and professional football players. Ted's brother Alex also achieved great celebrity as a television star after a stellar 12-year NFL career. But Alex's Detroit Lions teams never won the championship during his tenure. Playing on his championship status and punctuating his sibling rivalry with his celebrity brother, Ted said before the audience, "I'm a junior high school football coach and a physical education teacher and the amazing thing is my wife considers me a success."

In 1991, on the occasion of Bill Wade's wedding in Nashville, Tennessee, Bill, Ted, and I and our wives had a restaurant meal together. Ted picked up the check.

When my sons were in seventh and eighth grade, I was one of their football coaches, like Ted Karras.

It was an honor to have known Ted Karras. He made the world a better place.

Rudy Bukich's Funeral, March 9, 2016

"Rifle" Rudy Bukich played in the NFL for 14 seasons with the LA Rams, Pittsburgh Steelers, Washington Redskins, and Chicago Bears. Bukich played for the Bears from 1958-1959 and 1962-1968. He was backup quarterback for the Chicago Bears during their 1963 Championship Season. As a starter, the strong-arm Bukich was among the top quarterbacks in passing statistics in 1965-1966. During his college career at USC, Bukich landed some roles as an extra in the movies. He played a gladiator in Spartacus. He was also a popular sports reporter for ABC TV during his football career in Chicago.

Here are a few words that I said at Rudy Bukich funeral:

My name is Pat McCaskey. My grandfather, George Halas, was one of Rudy Bukich's football coaches.

Perhaps you're wondering what George Halas and Rudy Bukich have in common. They were both Most Valuable Players in the Rose Bowl: George Halas in 1919 and Rudy Bukich in 1953. Both of them worked for the Chicago Bears. Both of them were part of the Bears' 1963 NFL Championship Team.

In 1966, at a Bears' training camp practice at Saint Joseph's College in Rensselaer, Indiana, Rudy said to me, "See if you can throw a pass and hit the goalpost."

Then he threw. He got closer than I did.

On behalf of my family, thank you very much for Rudy's contributions to the Bears. We are very sorry for your loss.

Bill Wade's Funeral, April 30, 2016

Bill Wade was a great friend of mine. Here's what I said at his funeral:

Bill Wade was a great natural athlete who was very dedicated and very enthusiastic. He played on the football, basketball, and baseball teams while he attended Montgomery Bell Academy in Nashville, Tennessee. He was a single-wing tailback in football and a decent basketball player. He also played catcher, pitcher, shortstop, and center field for the baseball team.

Bill started at short during one particular game, but his team's starting pitcher that day walked the first six batters he faced in the first inning, and the team trailed 3–0. The coach summoned Bill to the mound. His sinker was devastating that day, and he ended up striking out 21 batters in a seven inning game. But his team was still losing 3–0 heading into the last inning, so Bill took matters into his own hands. He came to bat with the bases loaded and he hit a grand slam to give his team a 4–3 victory. His teammates carried him off the field on their shoulders.

After graduating from high school, Bill stayed in Nashville and he went to Vanderbilt University, where he quarterbacked the Commodores. He passed for 3,396 yards in his career—which stood as a school record for more than 30 years. He also earned second team All-America honors and he was named SEC Player of the Year in 1951.

Bill once threw a football 82 yards during a game against Arkansas. On that play, he scrambled behind the line of scrimmage; one of his receivers ran to the end zone, but he came back because he thought Bill couldn't throw the ball that far. But he did, and when the ball landed in the end zone right where the receiver had been standing, it ended up being an incomplete pass instead of a touchdown.

Bill did make the baseball team at Vanderbilt, but he didn't get to play much because he was involved in spring football practice. The Los Angeles Rams made him the first overall pick of the 1952 NFL Draft. After serving 2 years in the Navy, he received an offer to play baseball with the San Diego Padres of the Pacific Coast League during the Rams' off-seasons. However, the Rams wouldn't let him play pro baseball. Bill played for the Rams from 1954 through 1960; he was then traded to the Bears.

After the Bears won five straight to begin the 1963 season, we ended up suffering our first loss at San Francisco. During the flight home, Bill moved to the forward part of the plane and poured out his sorrows to Grandpa. Grandpa patiently listened and then he asked, "Who do we play next week?"

Later, Bill wrote that Grandpa had a "great ability to constantly push forward and look ahead through hardship and defeat, heartache and disappointment."

The Bears won the next four games, tied two, and won two more. Then we beat the New York Giants in the NFL Championship Game, 14–10, as Bill scored both touchdowns on quarterback sneaks.

In the summer of 1966, after two-a-day practices at the Bears' training camp, Bill took the time to tutor me in the fundamentals of quarterbacking. Before each session, he would reach down to the ground and find a four-leaf clover. That meant we would have a good workout. He also said, "Everyone I've ever tutored in quarterbacking became an All-American."

That was a confidence builder. Bill was an excellent teacher.

While I was playing quarterback during one high school practice, the backfield coach told me to throw my passes with the nose of the football down. I insisted that the nose of the football should be up. He asked me, "Who taught you that?"

As quietly and as respectfully as I could, I replied, "Bill Wade."

The coach gave way and I was allowed to throw the way that Bill had taught me. I was on a great team. We were 9–0 and we outscored our opponents 341–80. After the season, I was named to an All-American team.

Bill was the Bears' quarterback coach in 1967. During training camp one day, some of the ball boys got involved in a tremendous water fight in a bathroom at one of the team's dormitories. Shower stalls were plugged, and water overflowed. Bill walked into the melee, surveyed the situation, and calmly said, "If you put the washroom back into its original condition, I won't tell Coach Halas."

Everyone accepted his offer.

After the season, Grandpa asked Bill to call him on May 1 and tell him if he wanted to continue with the team. That day, Bill told Grandpa that he wanted to retire in order to spend more time at home because of family issues. Grandpa tried to talk him out of it, and said, "If you agree to come back, I think something wonderful will happen."

Bill said no thank you. Unbeknownst to Bill, Grandpa might have eventually handed him the job of coach. On May 27, 1968, Grandpa announced his retirement from coaching.

When I was a high school freshman, I didn't go to the Bears 1963 NFL Championship Game because I had basketball practice. When I used that as an illustration to my sons as to how dedicated they should be to their teams, they said, "Dad, you made a mistake."

A few years ago, Bill asked me to speak at his funeral. I was in the Bears' draft room on Thursday and Friday, but not today because of Bill's funeral. I didn't make a mistake this time either.

If the Apostles had played football, they would have been a great team like the 1963 Chicago Bears. Peter would have been the quarterback like Bill Wade.

Buddy Ryan's Funeral, July 1, 2016

Buddy Ryan coached in the NFL for 26 seasons. While working with the Chicago Bears as Defensive Coordinator, his "46" defense helped make the 1985 Bears one of the greatest on record and drove them to a Super Bowl XX win. I spoke at Buddy Ryan's Funeral Mass on July 1, 2016 at Saint Lawrence Church in Lawrenceburg, Kentucky.

There are several, famous Buddy Ryan quotes. I have translated parts of them into church language.

"My wife better shape up. There are a lot of people competing for her job.

"I bought my wife the best lawn mower and the best snow blower in the neighborhood.

"If I felt any better, I'd have to be two people.

"I've got the world by the rear on a downhill pull.

"If you don't want to work, you shouldn't have hired out.

"A shower can't hurt you and it might do you some good."

My favorite Buddy quote involves something very personal. In 1982, I gave a booklet of my writings to Buddy and his wife, Joannie, for Christmas. After Joannie had read them, she asked Buddy if I was going to become a priest. That was before I met my beloved wife in whom I am well pleased.

I said to Buddy, "The trouble with writing about your ideals is that you have to try and live up to them."

Buddy replied, "I know what you mean. Do you think it's easy for me to be a jerk all the time."

Buddy was full of bluster, but when I asked him to participate in a community involvement project, the only thing he asked me was, "Can I bring my wife?"

Neill Armstrong's Funeral, August 20, 2016

Here are my thoughts on Neill Armstrong at his funeral:

Neill Armstrong was head coach of the Chicago Bears from 1978 through 1981. When Neill was a player in the NFL from 1947 through 1951, for the Philadelphia Eagles, the Bears were one of the toughest opponents. In 1978, Neill told my grandfather, George Halas, that the Eagles' coach, Greasy Neale, taught the Eagles to give a little more effort to beat the Bears. Coach Halas's reply was "GOOOOOOOD!"

In 1980, Bob Thomas's brother, Rick, addressed the Bears' defense to explain the NFL's intricate system for making the playoffs. Prior to the lecture, Rick called the Bears' office and asked to speak with some of the coaches.

When he heard one of the coaches swearing with an Oklahoma accent, Rick was surprised until he found out it was Buddy Ryan and not Neill Armstrong.

When Neill was the head coach of the Bears, I was the Bears' public relations assistant. We worked very well together.

In 1981, the Bears had a half mile run to start training camp. I called it the Armstrong 880. One player, Kris Haines, finished ahead of me. He was later cut.

I only saw Neill mad one time. Some reporters were complaining about not having as much access to Neill as they wanted. Instead of swearing, Neill said, "That really gripes me."

After Neill had cooled off, he said, "Sometimes my newspaper isn't delivered."

I've had the good fortune to be associated with the Bears all my life. Neill Armstrong is the best man I've ever met.

Thoughts on Bill George

Bill George was born October 27, 1929 in Waynesburg, Pennsylvania. When he was on his recruiting trip to Wake Forest, they allegedly showed him the Duke campus. When he reported for freshmen football, he asked, *"What happened to all of those nice buildings that I saw on my recruiting trip?"* He was allegedly told, *"This is the freshmen campus. You'll be on the nicer campus next year."*

In 1951, he was a second round draft choice of the Bears. He played for the Bears from 1952 through 1965. In 1954, the Bears were in a 5-2 defense with Bill George at middle guard. After the other team had completed short, slant passes over the middle, he said to George Connor in the defensive huddle, *"If I drop back in the middle, I can make some interceptions."* George Connor replied, *"If you think you can do it, go ahead."* So Bill George dropped back in the middle, made interceptions, and created the 4-3 defense.

In 1961, the San Francisco 49ers won four of their first five games with a new formation, the shotgun. On Sunday, October 22, Bill George returned to his middle guard position, made several great plays, and the Bears won 31-0. Bill Wade threw four touchdown passes.

Bill Wade did not drink alcohol. So in training camp Bill George and Fred Williams planted alcohol in Bill Wade's room. Then they confronted him about his alleged hypocrisy.

In 1966, Bill George asked my father, Ed McCaskey, to look after Brian Piccolo. Then my parents adopted Brian Piccolo.

In 1974, my father presented Bill George for induction into the Pro Football Hall of Fame.

When you asked Bill George if he was capable of doing something, he would reply, "That was my major." When you asked Bill George for a favor, he would reply, "If you had asked anyone else, I would have been offended."

In 1975, Bill George and his sons, Leo and Biff, helped me move into my first apartment.

I'm a graduate of the Bill George Finishing School. He taught me to always say something positive. For example, when you're dancing with a girl who is overweight, you should say, "For a fat girl, you don't sweat much."

At the end of "Franny and Zooey," by J. D. Salinger, Zooey told Franny why their brother, Seymour, wanted him to shine his shoes before he went on the radio. "He said to shine them for the Fat Lady."

Zooey further said to Franny, "There isn't anyone out there who isn't Seymour's Fat Lady...don't you know what that Fat Lady really is? It's Christ Himself."

Edward W. McCaskey: Conscience

Edward W. McCaskey was born April 27, 1919 in Philadelphia. He played offensive tackle at Lancaster Catholic High School. He sang with dance bands for 3 years before enrolling at the University of Pennsylvania in 1940. While he was at Penn, he was elected class president, continued a singing career, and met Virginia Halas who was a student at Drexel. They were married February 2, 1943.

McCaskey served with the U.S. Army 80th Infantry in France in World War II. He enlisted as a private and left with a Captain's rank. After the War, McCaskey was in the music publishing business in New York. He was associated with the late Jimmy Dorsey. He was a merchandising manager for the National Retail Tea and Coffee Association, Executive Vice President of Merchandise Services, Inc., and an account executive for E. F. McDonald Co.

In 1967, McCaskey joined the Chicago Bears as Vice President and Treasurer. In 1983, he was named Chairman. On Thursday, June 2, 1988, he was the commencement speaker at Lancaster Catholic High School. He was Chairman Emeritus of the Bears from 1999 until his death on April 8, 2003.

McCaskey was a popular figure within the NFL and was referred to by many as the "conscience" of the League, as well as a sounding board for many of its leaders. He contributed to numerous charitable and civic organizations on behalf of the Bears and served as the guiding force behind the Brian Piccolo Fund.

Former Bears Director of Administration Bill McGrane wrote:

"When Ed McCaskey died in April, it seemed like we lost our voice. And a grand baritone it was. No one sings in the hall anymore. No one laughs like he did, or puts a firm hand on a rookie's shoulder and looks him in the eye when they meet quite like he did. He enjoyed meeting the rooks and they knew it. Ed loved his family, he loved the Bears, and he loved that he was able to entertain so many people. So did we."

Knock Mosaic

Chapter 15: More Pilgrimages

In a sense, our entire journey on earth is a pilgrimage towards redemption and God. It would take an encyclopedic work to cover all the formal pilgrimages that are worthy of consideration. However, we did want to include some information on a few more in this last chapter along with some sports and faith stories.

The Stations of the Cross

The Via Dolorosa or the "Way of Grief" is the path in the Old City of Jerusalem that follows the route that Jesus took to his crucifixion. In Catholic churches and other holy places all over the world are found the Stations of the Cross that give the faithful the experience of following the Way without extensive travel. Saint Leonard of Port Maurice spread the devotion of the Stations in the 18th century to churches.

Leonard was born in 1676 in Port Maurice on the northwestern coast of Italy. He joined the Franciscan

195

Friars Minor completing his studies at the College of Saint Bonaventura in Rome.[66] He intended to serve as a missionary to China, but he became seriously ill. His health did not return for 4 years. He became a great preacher and he held missions. In 1710, he founded the Monastery of Icontro in the mountains outside Florence. He and others would travel to conduct missions and return to the monastery to recover. Leonard preached retreats for over 40 years and he was one of the greatest speakers of his day.

Pope Clement XII (1730-1740) and Pope Benedict XIV (1740-1758) called Leonard to Rome for special assignments. He spread the devotion to the Sacred Heart of Jesus and the Blessed Sacrament. The Franciscans had long been custodians of the "Way of the Cross" and Leonard promoted the Stations and set them up at hundreds of locations across Italy. Despite his early illness, Leonard lived a long and arduous life. He died in 1751 at the age of 75. Pope Pius IX (1846-1878) pronounced Saint Leonard's canonization on June 29. 1867.

Lauren Hill's Cross

Many people meditate on the Stations of the Cross. They get a better appreciation of God's love for us and the price He paid for our salvation. The Stations also remind us that we must pick up our own cross and carry it as well. For some, suffering comes early in life. Lauren Hill was someone who picked up her cross and did her best to help us by her example.

---

[66] Now called the Pontifical University of St. Bonaventure, the school provides for the advanced study of theology by members of the Conventual branch of the Franciscan Order.

PILGRIMAGE

Lauren Hill reached an international audience in her fight against a rare brain cancer. The young athlete's efforts were advanced by her willingness to stand up and tell the community and the world about it—both on good days and on bad. Her courage and her never-give-up attitude were encouraging, heartwarming, and inspirational for everyone. With Lauren came grace.

As a senior in high school, she was diagnosed with a brain cancer called diffuse intrinsic pontine glioma (DIPG). The disease strikes approximately 300 children a year and much research is needed before a cure is likely to be found. Fund-raising efforts in Hill's name were begun to fight the disease.

The young athlete from the town of Greendale, Indiana, played soccer and basketball at Lawrenceburg High School in Lawrenceburg, Indiana. Lauren kept fighting on as she continued her education at Mount Saint Joseph University. She played games early in the season in 2014. The first game was a match between Mount Saint Joseph University and Hiram College held at Xavier University to accommodate the crowd. Over 10,000 tickets were sold in an hour!

Professional athletes came and paid tribute to Hill at various events. She had many friends who came by and received a smile that could light up any stadium, anywhere. While suffering, she fought the disease and was able to articulately disclose the effects of the disease on her to the medical community—something that was needed because often the disease attacks younger children, who are less likely to be able to describe their experiences.

Lauren Hill died on April 10, 2015. She will be remembered for many reasons and her fundraising efforts continue in her memory. Lauren's family worked with her and continue to support the fight against the disease. Over $2 million have been raised on Hill's behalf. Lauren lived one exemplary life and was inducted into the Sports Faith Hall of Fame posthumously in 2016.

Our Lady of Knock

Our Lady of Knock was a far different Marian Apparition than others that occurred in the 19th century. On the 21st of August, 1879, 15 people, from the village of Knock in County Mayo Ireland, witnessed an apparition of Our Lady, Saint Joseph, and Saint John the Evangelist at the south gable of Knock Parish Church. They prayed the rosary and watched the apparition for two hours in the rain before it faded away. The figures were white-like in appearance. There were no reports of any conversations at all by the viewers.

There have been reported cures of illnesses and ailments by those praying at the shrine and taking the local spring water. Two Commissions of Enquiry were held and the witnesses were interviewed and found to be "upright and trustworthy." On the day of the apparition, Archdeacon Cavanagh, the parish priest at Knock, had just celebrated his one hundredth Mass for the poor souls in purgatory.

The first organized pilgrimage to Knock took place in March 1880. County Mayo in western Ireland still has an unblemished beauty. It is the county of the classic movie, "The Quiet Man." The Potato Famine hit the area hard and some estimate that 100,000 people of the County died from the scourge. In 1979, Pope Saint John Paul visited the Knock Shrine during centenary celebrations. The Pope said, "I am here then as a pilgrim, a sign of the pilgrim Church throughout the world participating, through my presence as Peter's successor, in a very special way in the centenary celebration of this shrine." The Pope's visit had an impact and Knock became known internationally. Knock Basilica was built in 1976 and after the Pope's visit, an airport was opened in 1986. The Knock Basilica has undergone many enhancements recently.

My Favorite Childhood Trip

My paternal grandmother was Irish and "The Quiet Man" was a family favorite movie. My father's family was a mix of singers, scholars, and military men. As a child, occasionally I went on trips to see important places of faith and family. When I was 5 years old, my father and I travelled in a Pullman train from Chicago to Lancaster, Pennsylvania, my father's hometown. There was a compartment in the door where we left our shoes to be shined. I slept in the upper berth. After we had arrived in Lancaster, my Grandpa Dick gave me a large goldfish.

In front of my grandparents' home there were some brick stairs with cement inclined plane sides that I slid down repeatedly. This scuffed the backside of my grey pants with plaid lining. My cousins, Kay and Lisa, were also five, but they had been born 49 days earlier than I. They were smart enough not to slide down cement inclined planes.

I met my great Uncle Walter on that trip. He had played quarterback at the turn of the 19th century for Penn State. I wondered what a quarterback was. Uncle Walter dressed in a suit and a tie all the time.

Patrick McCaskey

Saint Peter's in the Loop

Many people in the Chicago area and for miles around have made a trip to downtown Chicago to pray, go to Mass, and Confession at Saint Peter's in the Loop. Saint Peter's is run by the Franciscans and it has long been a special pilgrimage place for Catholics to go to for renewal. The church is part of the urban landscape and its facade does little to attract attention. During work hours, thousands of loop employees file past on their way to jobs. You have to step back away from the building to see the cross overhead and if you stand on the other side of the street at night, the church's beautiful stained-glass windows tug at your heart gently in a humble way like Saint Francis himself.

George Halas

George Halas sits at his desk in the Chicago Bears office at 173 West Madison Street in Chicago. His hands folded, his head down, his lips moving slightly. It is Saturday afternoon in midsummer 1963. The office is nearly empty except for the "old man" himself, the club's chief executive everything. To a fly on the wall, it looks like George Stanley Halas is daydreaming. But the NFL titan's mind is clear. He is focused and as always, intense. He is thinking about what he has done wrong the past week. He is preparing himself for what all old-time Catholics called Confession.

Halas dons a simple felt fedora and walks a block over to Saint Peter's Church from his loop office and makes his way into a pew. In a few minutes the rest of the world disappears and he enters a quiet confessional.

Bless me Father for I have sinned. It has been one ...

He lays out his sins like he does every week. A kindly Franciscan Priest listens carefully, encourages Halas to do better and assigns a penance. As the Priests prays, Halas says his Act of Contrition:

Oh my God I am heartily sorry for having offended thee ...

Both priest and penitent finish their prayers at the same time. The priest gives him absolution and a blessing. George Stanley Halas crosses himself and as he steps out of the confessional; he suddenly feels like a kid again. The weight of the world is lifted and the crushing stress of his job seems to evaporate—at least for the time being. The man Bear fans call "Papa Bear" walks down the aisle of Saint Peter's towards a back pew. He knows the church so well that it is like another office. Saint Peter's is also a favorite church for cops, firemen, politicians, and thousands of other workers who have a kinship with Halas. In many ways, there is something about Saint Peter's in particular that fits Halas like a glove. Saint Peter's is a sturdy structure that is thickly solid at its base with big brass doors that greet churchgoers.

In a few minutes, Halas is back at his desk, hands in prayer, head down, and lips moving ever so slightly. He takes most of his prayers back with him, because he does not want to leave his faith in church. Rosary beads and prayer are part and parcel of George Stanley Halas's life and they are not incongruous with the pushing, the shoving, the steel determination, and effort that he puts into running his team. Oh, Halas will likely go over the edge with his cussing or anger, and maybe he suspects that. He will be right back in the confessional and do his best to set it all right.

After he finishes his penance, he adds an extra prayer.

Lord let me win another championship this year. You know the boys deserve it.

Patrick McCaskey

My Surprise Confession

In 1966, when I was a Notre Dame High School senior, I threw some interceptions at away games. Fifty years later, I'm still working off Father Corcoran's penance. I like to receive the Sacrament of Reconciliation at Saint Peter's Church on Madison Street in Chicago. I slip in a side door and disguise my voice.

On Wednesday, December 11, 2013, I went to Notre Dame College Prep for what I thought was going to be an all school Mass in the gym. My favorite part of being an alumnus is going to the all school Masses. They are a preview of heaven.

Instead of an all school Mass, there was a mass reconciliation. There were 15 priests to administer the Sacrament of Reconciliation. It was a preview of purgatory. Pride is a sin. So I don't say that I am proud to be an alumnus. I am grateful. Father Conyers believes that over 400 Dons received the Sacrament of Reconciliation that day.

Unbeheaded

If John the Baptist had not been beheaded,
What would his life have been like?
Would he have been one
Of the Apostles?
Would he have continued to bellow
Or would he have become mellow
Like Christ?
When Christ talked
With His Father,
Would John have been allowed
To hear?
He was not known as a listener.
Would he have stopped calling everyone
A brood of vipers?

PILGRIMAGE

Would he have sent Boy Scouts
Looking for snipes?
Would he have passed up loaves and fishes
For honey and locusts?
If John the Baptist had not been beheaded
He might have been the original Bishop Sheen.
—Patrick McCaskey

My Fellow Pilgrim, Coach Gordon

Coach Gordon, the founding pastor of Lawndale Community Church is a good family friend of mine. He is an inspiration to many people. When I think about Coach and Anne Gordon, and my wife, Gretchen, and I, I hear the opening lines of "Romeo and Juliet" and I rewrite them.

Two households, both alike in dignity
In Chicagoland, where we lay our scene
From Bible love witness to God's glory
Where FCA makes LC3 quite clean[67]
From forth the families of these great friends
A pair of God-blessed marriages live life
Whose adventurous giddiness pillows lends
Doth with their love enhance the ideal wife
The wonderful passage of their Christ-centered love
And the continuance of their parents' age
Which but their children's growth, we should behoove
Is now the fifteen minutes of our stage
The which if you with patient ears attend

---

[67] FCA is Fellowship of Christian Athletes and LC3 is Lawndale Christian Community Church, which was started by Coach Gordon and local community members on the West Side of Chicago.

Patrick McCaskey

What here shall miss, our toil shall strive to mend
—Patrick McCaskey

My Apocryphal Meeting with the Trinity

After high school, I had to give up playing football because of severe eye problems. The next seven paragraphs are apocryphal.

I went for a walk along the shore of Lake Michigan. When I found a dead horse on the beach, I kicked it, but rigor mortis had set in and I hurt my foot.

Suddenly The Blessed Trinity appeared to me. I asked Them what I should do now. Should I try to be Archbishop of Chicago?

Jesus Christ put his hand on my shoulder compassionately and said, "You were not meant to be a celibate."

Then God the Father said, "I want you to work for the Chicago Bears. By the time you finish college, they will need your help. I have also given you the talent to be a writer. If you don't use it, I'll break your arm in three places."

I asked God the Father, "What about performing collections of my greatest works?"

God the Father said, "I'll let you know about that later. The most important thing for you is to do what's right or else The Holy Spirit won't inspire you."

Then all Three of Them disappeared.

More Than Winning

"If you put these instructions before the brethren, you will be a good minister of Christ Jesus, nourished on the words of the faith and of the good doctrine which you have followed. Have nothing to do with godless and silly myths. Train yourself in godliness; for while bodily training is of some value, godliness is of value in every way, as it holds promise for the present life and also for the life to come."

1 Timothy 4:6-8

What we need,
God provides.
What we want
Is another story,
Not necessarily a Cinderella one.
When in doubt,
Take it to a higher court.
Pray about it.
Don't despair.
Once you stop trying,
Things get worse in a hurry.
Loving is more than winning.
So is forgiving.
Our mandate is
To love God and each other.
In our attempts to love,
We are often funny.
As far as I know,
All my apologies are up-to-date.
—Patrick McCaskey

Patrick McCaskey

Conclusion

"You could say our lives are a pilgrimage—an effort to unite the spirit to the work of the flesh. As you are making the journey with your body, your soul is part of that, and as you walk along with others you create community..."[68]

—*Martin Sheen*

I have been writing about sports and faith for over 40 years now. I think sports is in many ways akin to a pilgrimage. And by training and discipline, athletes seek out something greater. They are like trekkers who take long faithful journeys seeking to find themselves and their God. Faithful athletes use their God-given talents to seek the greater glory of God. And it is seldom easy. But it is easy to lose their way.

Many Cathedrals soar high in the sky with thin walls adorned with stained glass. Scholar Roland Bainton wrote that Cathedrals showing the glory of creation with flowers and foliage also have gargoyles and images of dark minions. The Cathedrals express all those forces battling for man's soul. "Tranquility is not granted on this earthly pilgrimage."[69] We are reminded that our own personal pilgrimage on earth will pit many forces that will affect our spiritual journey. Like the trekkers on the Camino, may your journey lead you to find God and peace.

---

[68] Jo Siedlecka, "A father and son project: Martin Sheen, Emilio Estevez discuss The Way." *Independent Catholic News*, February 24, 2011, viewed at http://www.indcatholicnews.com/news.php?viewStory=17731 on May 24, 2016.

[69] Roland H. Bainton, Christianity (An American Heritage Library) (Boston: Houghton Mifflin, 1964, 1987) 185.

PILGRIMAGE

Voice Mail Message

Hello.

This is Pat McCaskey.

I grew up in Des Plaines, Illinois.

Des Plaines is the city of destiny:

Decency, dignity, and determination.

Illinois is the land of Lincoln.

Lincoln is the greatest president

In the history of the United States.

The United States is the greatest nation

In the history of the world.

God created the world in six days.

In God we trust.

I'm calling from Lake Forest, Illinois.

Lake Forest is the city of trees.

Joyce Kilmer wrote a poem called "Trees."

Illinois is the land of Lincoln.

I repeated that for emphasis.

We only have forty seconds

To put the ball in play.

I guess I'm out of time.

Appendix

Destiny[70]

In the movie "Young Frankenstein," Gene Wilder exclaimed, "Destiny, destiny, no escaping that for me." This is a work of fiction. The players were named after the apostles. Thanks to Clair Bee, we know that "nicknames win ball games."[71]

To prepare for the Destiny High School varsity football season, our quarterback, Pete, ran five miles a day, six days a week. He took Sundays off.

One of the things that kept him going during those runs was the possibility that someday I, Paul the team manager, might tell the story. I guess today's the day.

Pete worked for his parish that summer. He mowed the lawns and he painted classrooms.

At the end of the summer, the pastor paid him and asked him, "Now what are you going to do with all of this money?"

Pete replied, "I don't know."

The pastor asked, "Why don't you give it to the orphanage?"

Pete quoted his mother and replied, "We'll see."

Pete and his teammate, end, Tom, went to football camp together. They did all the fitness workouts that their coaches had assigned to them.

[70] This is a sports and faith story including part of speeches from Patrick McCaskey's presentations.
[71] Dennis Gildea, *Hoop Crazy: The Lives of Clair Bee and Chip Hilton* (Fayetteville: University of Arkansas, 2013) 111.

Pete also did some more besides. He read the books on his summer book list: *Life with Father*, by Clarence Day; *The Homecoming*, by Earl Hamner; *"The Southpaw,"* by Mark Harris; *"My Life and Hard Times,"* by James Thurber; and *"One Man's Meat,"* by E. B. White.

When Pete and Tom reported for three-a-day practices at Destiny High School, they were ready. So were their coaches and their teammates. Pete won the football players' 600-yard run in 1:21.8.

The defense was four linemen, four linebackers, two defensive backs, and one safety. The team used an option offense, a scheme that focused on timing, trickery, and instant decisions that had to be made with great discipline.

The Destiny Team

E/LB	Tom	6-4	195
E/S	Andy	6-2	190
T/DT	Phil	6-2	240
T/DT	Simon	6-2	225
G/DE	Bart	6-4	215
G/DE	Ted	6-1	210
C/LB	Seamus	6-1	205
QB/LB	Pete	6-1	190
B/LB	Hew	5-11	201
B/DB	Jim	6-0	180
B/DB	John	6-0	170
K/P	Matt	6-1	190

When I complained to Father Expert, the team chaplain, about all the work that I had to do as the manager, he quoted Scottish evangelist Oswald Chambers: "The worth of a man is revealed in his attitude to ordinary things when he is not before the footlights."

At the initial meeting with the parents and the players, Coach Francis, who like our Pope was named after Saint Francis of Assisi, reviewed the "Ten Commandments of Football."

First, he pointed out a little history. "On Friday, September 17, 1920, the original meeting for what is now the National Football League took place at Ralph Hay's Hupmobile Showroom in Canton, Ohio. That's why the Pro Football Hall of Fame is located there. There weren't enough chairs for Hay and George Halas and the other founders. So they sat on the fenders and the running boards of the cars. The Ten Commandments of Football was created based on the original meeting and the history of the game that followed."

The Commandments

I.   Football is a wonderful game. There's blocking and tackling and much, much more. Be enthusiastic.

II. Weddings, births, and vacations should take place during the off-seasons.

III. Remember the Hupmobile and the original meeting.

IV. All previous games are preparation for the next one.

V.   Obey the personal conduct policy.

VI. Work for the good of the league.

VII. Win championships with sportsmanship.

VIII. You shall not criticize the officials.

IX. You shall not covet other teams' coaches or players.

X.   Game times are tentative and subject to flexible scheduling.

The preseason went by quickly. After the last preseason practice, Father Expert suggested to Coach Francis, "You could always call it a rebuilding year."

Coach Francis confidently said, "We've built."

To the newspapers, Coach Francis said, "We have a balanced offensive attack this year and can rely on both passing and running to score. Defensively, we're quicker and much more experienced than last year. It's up to the kids, if they want to win, and work hard for success, we have the talent to be one of the best teams Destiny has ever seen."

Seamus and Tom were elected co-captains.

At the all-school pep rally in the gym before the first game, Father Expert prayed a football prayer.

Bitterness is spiritual cancer.

Forgiveness is spiritual rapture.

Weather is a reminder that God is The Boss.

The Spirit strengthens us even after a loss.

Jesus Christ is The Man;

Salvation is the plan.

When we dance God's dance,

He gives us another chance.

God's work is efficient;

His food is sufficient.

Here's a part of my prayers;

Coach and play without swears.

Coach Francis came up to the mic and said, "We have a great program at Destiny and it will get better this year. We want to win championships with sportsmanship. We do good works quietly, for God's glory. We fear God and we respect our opponents. We are trying to keep Destiny High School going until The Second Coming. We work diligently and we trust God for the results. Like the Magi who followed the great star, we go forward in faith.

"We are grateful for at least the following: God created a wonderful world in six days; Jesus died for our sins, including fumbles; when we need The Holy Spirit, He is there. He is even there when we think that we don't need Him.

"We are hopeful that the world will not end until Destiny High School has the most championships. We want to play our games with cooperation that is like an Amish barn-raising. We go to Mass and Bible Study and have daily devotions. Our mandate is to love God and each other. In our attempts to love, we are often funny.

"Destiny High School is a place of work and not a den of thieves. It is a halfway house to heaven. Instead of saying, "Please be quiet,' we say 'Please become a mime.' We give away the credit and we take the blame. We criticize privately and we praise publicly. Instead of singing as soloists, we sing as a chorus. We provide accountability and positive reinforcement for each other.

"Goethe once said that you must labor to possess what you have inherited. 'If we are not grateful for our gifts and opportunities, we are not likely to value them, and if we do not value them, we are not likely to work hard to preserve and improve them.'[72] If you know some people who are not yet Destiny High School fans, don't be discouraged. Some of the greatest Christians started

---

[72] William Bennett, *The Moral Compass* (New York: Simon and Schuster, 1995).

out as atheists. Jesus forgave the good thief. All they have to do is repent.

"Our football stadium is our largest classroom. What did William Shakespeare's father say to William Shakespeare? '*Make plays.*' Let our football stadium be a reminder: God performs miracles for people of faith who diligently work together."

On Friday, September 16, we played the Natives at Destiny Stadium. In the first quarter, Jim was halfback and he went in motion to the right.

Pete pivoted left and handed off to Jim who took it up the middle and raced past pursuing Natives for 52 yards and a touchdown.

In the second quarter, after a long drive, Hew powered in for a 1-yard touchdown.

In the third quarter, John dazzled the crowd with a 67-yard punt return. Jim motored in on a 2-yard touchdown run.

After a long drive, John finished another scoring drive on a 1-yard run. In the fourth quarter, John scampered in on a 19-yard touchdown run. Hew finished things off with a 2-yard touchdown run. Matt was 6-for-6 on extra points.

We won, 42–19.

On Friday, September 23, we played the Indians at Destiny Stadium.

With no score at half, we gathered at the south end of Destiny Stadium.

Coach Francis said to us, "You have a chance to be one of the best Destiny teams. The second half will be remembered for many years to come."

The second half was another defensive struggle. We scored in the third quarter on Matt's 20-yard field goal.

In the fourth quarter, an Indians punt came Jim's way. Andy took out two tacklers with one fierce block allowing Jim to get behind a wall of Destiny blockers, he scooted up the right sideline 64-yards.

Two plays later, Hew scored from 1-yard out.

We won, 9–0.

On Friday, September 30, we played the Romans at Destiny Stadium.

In the first quarter, after the offense moved into scoring position, Hew ran off tackle on a 3-yard touchdown run.

Later, Pete ran around Andy on an option play for 82 yards and a score.

In the second quarter, Hew with Phil in front of him, took it in from the 2.

With 10 seconds left in the first half, Pete faked a handoff to Hew and then rolled left, faked the pass and ran 36 yards for a touchdown.

In the third quarter after another long drive, Jim ran outside for 1 yard and a touchdown.

Jim sprinted 55-yards down the sideline on a punt return. On the next play, he ran the final 2 yards for a touchdown.

In the fourth quarter, Simon had a 57-yard kickoff return. Two plays later, Pete faked a handoff to Hew, rolled right on an option play and ran 9 yards for a touchdown.

Hew intercepted a pass and returned it 45 yards for a touchdown.

Matt kicked 6 extra points on the day and we won, 54–13.

Coach Francis told reporters. "Matt is the best kicker we've had at Destiny. He does all our punting and kicking. It's been our kicking plus a strong defense that has enabled us to stay unbeaten after our first three games. Anyone who saw our game with the Indians will testify to that.

"Our defense was tremendous. We held the Indians to 111 yards on the ground and seven first downs. It was the first time we beat the Indians."

On Saturday, October 8, we played the Corinthians at their homecoming and they were also 3–0. It was very hot. Several players reported that when the Corinthians Chain Crew was moving the chains they were singing "That's the sound of the men, working on the chain, ga-ang" by Sam Cooke.

In the first quarter, Phil and Bart rushed the Corinthian Quarterback and Ted intercepted the pass and ran it back 46 yards for a touchdown. Matt kicked the extra point.

In the second quarter, Matt kicked a 30-yard field goal. After a scoreless third quarter, Hew had a 2-yard touchdown run to cap off a long drive. Matt kicked the extra point.

We won, 17–7.

On Friday, October 14, we played the Galatians at Destiny Stadium. It was our homecoming.

In the first quarter, we drove the length of the field on a long series and Hew scored on a 1-yard touchdown run. John had a beautiful 20-yard touchdown run.

In the second quarter, Hew had an 8-yard touchdown run.

In the third quarter, Bart and Ted rushed a Galatian Quarterback pass that Phil intercepted and ran back 38 yards for a score.

In the fourth quarter, Jim topped off a long series with a 3-yard touchdown run. Matt kicked 4 extra points that day.

We won, 34–6.

Coach Francis said to reporters, "Phil continually amazes me. He's a top blocker and our leading tackler but the greatest thing about him is his ability to exert a second and third effort. Time and again this season, he has recovered from the initial block on him to stop the ball-carrier.

"This is a rough league and we've taken a tremendous physical beating in every game this fall."

On Friday, October 21, we played the Ephesians on a cold and windy night at Destiny Stadium.

In the first quarter, Pete faked a handoff with Simon in front blocking, rolled right and threw an 11-yard touchdown pass to John.

Later in the quarter, we ran another option pass. Pete faked to Hew, rolled right, and threw a 19-yard touchdown pass to John.

In the third quarter, Pete faked to Hew, rolled right, and threw 43-yards to John for the "hat trick." Still later in the quarter, Pete faked to Hew, rolled right, faked a pass to John, and ran 24 yards for a touchdown. Later, the defense scored when Ted blocked a punt that Hew recovered and ran back 24 yards for a touchdown.

More scoring followed when John sped past defenders on a 12-yard touchdown run.

In the fourth quarter, Hew had an 18-yard touchdown run. Matt kicked a perfect 7 extra points that day and we won, 49–7.

On Sunday, October 30, we played the Philippians in an away game. It was cold, but we started out red hot. John returned the kickoff 75-yards for a touchdown.

Later in the first quarter, Pete threw a 9-yard touchdown pass to Andy

In the second quarter, Pete had a 2-yard quarterback sneak for a touchdown.

Later in the second quarter, Pete threw a 7-yard touchdown pass to Jim. To start the second half in spectacular fashion, John caught the kickoff and handed off to Jim who ran 96 yards for a touchdown passing right in front of the Philippian bench. In the fourth quarter, Pete threw a 27-yard touchdown pass to Tom. Tom was not finished and a short time later he blocked a punt, recovered the ball, and ran 20 yards for a touchdown. Pete threw a 20-yard touchdown pass to Andy. Matt kicked 6 extra points on the day and we won, 54–16.

After the game, Coach Francis said to reporters, "Our players set their mind to a high goal; they made sacrifices all season to train. We have good material and depth. Students, faculty, and administration are behind us, win or lose. Everybody here cares. We've had great play from Bart, Ted, Pete, Lawson, and a number of others."

On Friday, November 4, we played the Colossians away.

In the first quarter, Pete faked to Hew with Simon making space for him, rolled right, and completed a 12-yard pass to John. Hew finished the drive off with a 4-yard touchdown run. On another long series, Pete snuck up the middle on a 5-yard touchdown run.

In the second quarter, Matt kicked a field goal.

In the third quarter, Hew exploded for a 74-yard touchdown run. Pete dropped back and threw a 16-yard touchdown pass in traffic to Andy. John snuck in an interception that he ran back 27 yards for a TD. In the fourth quarter, Pete handed off to Hew, who ran 6 yards for a touchdown.

We did not punt at all in the game. Matt was perfect on the day with 6 extra points and a field goal. We won, 45–0.

On Friday, November 11, we played the Thessalonians at Destiny Stadium on Senior Day. Before the game, parents of the seniors lined up with their sons on the Destiny sideline and were introduced.

In the first quarter, Pete ran up the middle on a quarterback sneak for 1 yard and a touchdown.

The Thessalonians' punter recovered a long snap in the end zone where Hew tackled him for a safety.

Late in the quarter, Hew ran up the middle for a 1-yard touchdown run. In the second quarter, Jim ran up the middle and then down the right sideline 76 yards for a touchdown. The Destiny Team never let up. With 25 seconds left in the half, Pete threw a 19-yard touchdown pass to John. In the fourth quarter, Pete completed a 33-yard pass to Hew over the middle. After the catch, Hew ran 50 yards for a touchdown. Matt was perfect on the day with 5 extra points. We won 37–12.

We were 9–0 and outscored our opponents 341–80. Our opponents did not score any points in the third quarter. We won our first five games by an average score of 31–9. We outscored opponents 156–45. We won our last four games by an average score of 46–9. We outscored opponents 185–35. The average score for the season was 38–9.

For the season, we had 31 rushing touchdowns, 10 passing touchdowns, and 7 return touchdowns.

On Tuesday, November 15, there was a public address announcement at Destiny High School. "Congratulations to the following football players who were named to the All-Suburban Catholic Conference Team: Tom at linebacker, Phil at defensive tackle, Hew at fullback, Bart at defensive end, John at safety, Pete at quarterback, and Andy at end."

On Friday, November 18, the Destiny seniors and the freshmen played the juniors and the sophomores at Destiny Stadium. Before the final whistle blew to end the season, the team set its sights on the traditional inter squad game. Another lesson from the Pros would surface.

In 1950, the Cleveland Browns beat the Philadelphia Eagles 35–10. After the game, the Eagles' coach, Greasy Neale, said that the Browns were a pass-only team. Browns' coach, Paul Brown, sought retribution by defeating the Eagles, 13–7, in their second meeting of the year without throwing a single pass.

Right before the kickoff, Coach Francis said to Pete, "You can pass as much as you want."

Pete thought, "I'll show him. We'll run it every play."

To start the game, Matt kicked off to the juniors and the sophomores. On their possession, they quickly ran for a touchdown run and kicked the extra point.

Pete got very angry. Some of the seniors were not comfortable trailing. He hollered at his teammates in the huddle to take the game seriously or we wouldn't win. Seamus had an interesting rebuttal. He said, "Don't worry about it; we're going to win."

John and Hew took turns carrying the ball behind wedge blocking behind Ted. When Ted needed a break, Pete called for wedge blocking behind Bart.

In many huddles, Hew told the offensive linemen that the blocking was great. Phil was grateful for the recognition.

The seniors started to warm up. In the first quarter, Hew had a touchdown run.

In the second quarter, Hew had a touchdown run.

In the third quarter, Pete called an option play, he faked to Hew and ran it around end for a touchdown.

In the fourth quarter, there were many substitutions. The coaches did not sing "Send in the Clowns." The seniors and the freshmen won 21–7. Matt as usual was spot on with his 3 extra points.

On Sunday, November 20, there was a team meeting in the Destiny High School cafeteria. We decided that everyone would letter because it was a championship team. The seniors got to keep their jerseys because it was a championship team. We voted for the most valuable player award.

On Tuesday, November 22, the fall sports banquet took place in the Destiny High School cafeteria. Tom was the most valuable player. He was a cross between Dick Butkus and Jonathan Winters. He led the team in tackles and he did impersonations from "The Wizard of Oz." He was dedicated and he was funny.

On Thursday, December 15, there was a banquet at a hotel for all of the all-conference high school football players in the state.

On Friday, December 23, the Catholic All Area team was announced. Phil and Pete were on it.

On Friday, January 6, the Catholic All American team was announced. Phil and Pete were on it.

The seniors on the football team went on a retreat together. Pete received a letter from his father.

PILGRIMAGE

Dear Son,

Now you are a high school senior and you are on your senior retreat. You are a very good student. You are on your way to a faith-based college where you can get an excellent education.

Most importantly, let's hope you're on your way to heaven. Regardless of where you go to college, let's keep the ultimate goal in mind. We're interested in schools that emphasize faith, education, and sports. We want to win championships with sportsmanship and we want to get to heaven. I'll be with you at the family retreat Mass.

It's important to grow physically, socially, culturally, and spiritually.

Physically, you are a very good athlete.

Socially, you are a very good family member and a very good friend.

Culturally, you are doing very well in school.

Spiritually, you go to Church and you exhibit sportsmanship. I want you to continue to be a servant leader like Jesus Who washed the feet of His Apostles. You are my beloved son in whom I am well pleased.

Jesus is my role model and I hope and trust that He is yours. Regardless of what others do, we need to do what is right.

We have God's grace and mercy that provide strength. Church and Bible Study and daily devotions keep us on the right path.

Your mother and I are praying that you will continue to grow in the Lord. If you are not called to the priesthood, I hope that you will marry a follower of Jesus, someone like your mother.

I enjoy being with you. You are very good company.

Pride is a sin. So I don't say that I am proud of you. I am grateful that you are my son. Thank you. I love you. It's great to be with you.

Your earthly father,

Photo Credits

All photographs are reproduced with permission (unless public domain).

Page	Photo Description	Source
Cover	McCaskey Travel	Author's Personal Photo
Page 1	El Camino Pilgrims Record	Public Domain
Page 8	Bear Woznick	Bear Woznick
Page 14	Annunciation of Man's Salvation, painting from the Dominican Church in Vittoriosa, Malta.	Fr. Lawrence Lew, O.P. Creative Commons (CC BY-NC-ND 2.0) https://flic.kr/p/FeJ6Ky
Page 17	Catholic Mass in the Grotto of the Annunciation	Berthold Werner, Wikipedia Public Domain. See https://en.wikipedia.org/wik i/Basilica_of_the_Annunciat ion#/media/File:Nazaret_Ve rkuendigungsbasilika_BW_9 .JPG
Page 25	April Ortenzo	Tim Hipps, U.S. Army Installation Management Command
Page 30	Saint Peter's Dome from the Vatican Gardens	Fr. Lawrence Lew, O.P. Creative Commons (CC BY-NC-ND 2.0) See https://flic.kr/p/ff2iti
Page 35	The Mother Church, Saint John's Lateran facade	Fr. Lew Lawrence, O.P. Creative Commons (CC BY-NC-ND 2.0) See https://flic.kr/p/8ApKxo
Page 38	Saint Peter and Saint Paul with Our Lord, mosaic at front of Basilica of Saint Paul Outside the Walls,	Fr. Lawrence Lew, O.P. Creative Commons (CC BY-NC-ND 2.0) See https://flic.kr/p/AgKrLK

Page 42	Morley Frasor	Frank Passi, Albion Michigan Historian
Page 45	Church of the Visitation at Ein Karem	© Berthold Werner, Wikimedia Commons / CC-BY-SA-3.0 / GFDL. See https://commons.wikimedia.org/wiki/File:Ein_Karem_BW_5.jpg, photo is unaltered by printed in black and white.
Page 50	Sister Mariam James Heidland, S.O.L.T.	Sister Mariam James Heidland, S.O.L.T.
Page 53	Children of Fatima	Photojournalist Joshua Benoliel.
Page 62	Lourdes at Dawn	Fr. Lawrence Lew, O.P. Creative Commons (CC BY-NC-ND 2.0) See https://flic.kr/p/2T5ndD
Page 65	Saint Bernadette from Lourdes-Lower Basilica, Glass Art (Gemmail)	Fr. Lawrence Lew, O.P. Creative Commons (CC BY-NC-ND 2.0) See https://flic.kr/p/7TXmTx
Page 69	Haley Scott DeMaria	Haley Scott DeMaria
Page 77	Saint Francis Assisi from Holy Trinity Stratford on the Avon	Fr. Lew Lawrence, O.P. Creative Commons (CC BY-NC-ND 2.0) See https://flic.kr/p/9phApU
Page 80	Sister Rita Clare Yoches	Sister Rita Clare Yoches
Page 92	Statue of Kateri Tekakwitha	Basilica of Sainte-Anne-de-Beaupré by LovesMacs, Creative Commons (CC BY-SA 3.0). See: https://commons.wikimedia.org/wiki/File:Kateri_Tekakwitha_au_Qu%C3%A9bec.JPG

Page 95	Saint Isaac Jogues	Oil portrait by Donald Guthrie McNab, Public Domain in United States.
Page 103	Saint Thomas Aquinas and the Eucharist, painting at St Dominic's House (House of Pierre Seilhan in Toulouse)	Fr. Lawrence Lew, O.P. Creative Commons (CC BY-NC-ND 2.0) See https://flic.kr/p/tahg4u
Page 107	Canterbury Cathedral, the Empty Shrine	Fr. Lawrence Lew, O.P. Creative Commons (CC BY-NC-ND 2.0) See https://flic.kr/p/qix6CK
Page 114	Mike Fitzgibbons	Carmel High School
Page 124	Mark Twain at Oxford	Photo from Wikimedia Commons. See https://commons.wikimedia.org/wiki/File:Mark_Twain_DLitt.jpg.
Page 126	Waltons	CBS Publicity Photo from Wikimedia Commons. See https://commons.wikimedia.org/wiki/File:Waltons_1972.JPG
Page 127	Amish Life	Library of Congress, Carol Highsmith
Page 133	Rock Cut Farm	Library of Congress, Carol Highsmith
Page 144	Ziggy Czarobski	University of Notre Dame Athletic Communications
Page 147	Virgin of Guadalupe, National Shrine, DC.	Fr. Lawrence Lew, O.P. Creative Commons (CC BY-NC-ND 2.0) See https://flic.kr/p/yQcj1p

Page 158	Scherpenheuvel Basilica	Belgium Scherpenheuvel Basilica by Paul Hermans, CC BY-SA 3.0 License. See: https://en.wikipedia.org/wik i/File:Scherpenheuvel_basili ek.jpg Photo is unaltered.
Page 168	Pope Francis, President Obama, Catholic School Children and Others	U.S. State Department Photo.
Page 195	Mosaic of Knock Apparition by PJ Lynch, Travisanutto Mosaics	Knock Shrine

Index